Shakespeare

at Peace

In the current climate of global military conflict and terrorism, *Shakespeare at Peace* offers new readings of Shakespeare's plays, illuminating a discourse of peace previously shadowed by war and violence. Using contemporary examples such as speeches, popular music, and science fiction adaptations of the plays, *Shakespeare at Peace* reads Shakespeare's work to illuminate current debates and rhetoric around conflict and peace. In this challenging and evocative book, Garrison and Pivetti re-frame Shakespeare as a proponent of peace, rather than war, and suggest new ways of exploring the vitality of Shakespeare's work for politics today.

John S. Garrison is Associate Professor of English at Grinnell College, USA.

Kyle Pivetti is Associate Professor of English at Norwich University, USA.

Spotlight on Shakespeare

Series Editors: John S. Garrison and Kyle Pivetti

Spotlight on Shakespeare offers a series of concise, lucid books that explore the vital purchase of the modern world on Shakespeare's work. Authors in the series embrace the notion that emergent theories, contemporary events, and movements can help us shed new light on Shakespeare's work and, in turn, his work can help us better make sense of the contemporary world. The aim of each volume is two-fold: to show how Shakespeare speaks to questions in our world and to illuminate his work by looking at it through new forms of human expression. *Spotlight on Shakespeare* will adopt fresh scholarly trends as contemporary issues emerge, and it will continually prompt its readers to ask, "What can Shakespeare help us see? What can he help us do?"

Spotlight on Shakespeare invites scholars to write non-exhaustive, pithy studies of very focused topics – with the goal of creating books that engage scholars, students, and general readers alike.

Available in this series:

Shakespeare at Peace
John S. Garrison and Kyle Pivetti

For more information about this series, please visit: www.routledge.com/Spotlight-on-Shakespeare/book-series/SOSHAX

JOHN S. GARRISON
AND KYLE PIVETTI

Shakespeare
at Peace

LONDON AND NEW YORK

First published 2019
by Routledge
2 Park Square, Milton Park, Abingdon, Oxon OX14 4RN

and by Routledge
52 Vanderbilt Avenue, New York, NY 10017

Routledge is an imprint of the Taylor & Francis Group, an informa business

© 2019 John S. Garrison and Kyle Pivetti

The right of John S. Garrison and Kyle Pivetti to be identified as authors of this work has been asserted by them in accordance with sections 77 and 78 of the Copyright, Designs and Patents Act 1988.

All rights reserved. No part of this book may be reprinted or reproduced or utilised in any form or by any electronic, mechanical, or other means, now known or hereafter invented, including photocopying and recording, or in any information storage or retrieval system, without permission in writing from the publishers.

Trademark notice: Product or corporate names may be trademarks or registered trademarks, and are used only for identification and explanation without intent to infringe.

British Library Cataloguing-in-Publication Data
A catalogue record for this book is available from the British Library

Library of Congress Cataloging-in-Publication Data
Names: Garrison, John S., 1970– author. | Pivetti, Kyle, author.
Title: Shakespeare at peace / John Garrison, Kyle Pivetti.
Description: Abingdon, Oxon ; New York, NY : Routledge, 2019. | Series: Spotlight on Shakespeare | Includes bibliographical references and index.
Identifiers: LCCN 2018023062 | ISBN 9781138230880 (hardback : alk. paper) | ISBN 9781138230897 (paperback : alk. paper) | ISBN 9781315316604 (Master) | ISBN 9781315316581 (ePub) | ISBN 9781315316598 (web pdf) | ISBN 9781315316574 (mobikindle)
Subjects: LCSH: Shakespeare, William, 1564–1616—Political and social views. | Peace in literature. | Politics in literature.
Classification: LCC PR3017 .G27 2019 | DDC 822.3/3—dc23
LC record available at https://lccn.loc.gov/2018023062

ISBN: 978-1-138-23088-0 (hbk)
ISBN: 978-1-138-23089-7 (pbk)
ISBN: 978-1-315-31660-4 (ebk)

Typeset in Joanna MT and Din
by Apex CoVantage, LLC

Printed and bound in Great Britain by
TJ International Ltd, Padstow, Cornwall

For Chris and Gail.

Contents

Note on texts viii
List of illustrations ix
Acknowledgments x

Introduction: the tide of war is receding   **1**

What's so funny 'bout peace, love, and understanding? One   **34**

Make love, not war Two   **63**

Flower power Three   **87**

Blowin' in the wind Four   **112**

Another world was possible Five   **141**

Afterword: war is not the answer   **177**

Further reading 186
Index 191

Note on texts

All quotations from Shakespeare's plays and poems are taken from *The Norton Shakespeare: Based on the Oxford Edition*, ed. Stephen Greenblatt, Walter Cohen, Jean E. Howard, and Katharine Eisaman Maus, 2nd edn. (New York: W. W. Norton & Company, 2008). Unless otherwise noted, all spelling and punctuation from early modern texts have been modernized.

Illustrations

I.1	*Coriolanus*, Dir. Fiennes, Icon Entertainment International and BBC Films, 2011.	17
1.1	Elvis Costello and the Attractions, "(What's So Funny 'Bout) Peace, Love, and Understanding," Dir. Statler, Columbia Records, 1979.	35
1.2	*Much Ado About Nothing*, Dir. Branagh, BBC Films, 1993.	37
2.1	"Love Is a Battlefield," Dir. Giraldi, GASP! Productions, 1983.	64
2.2	Title page, *Venus and Adonis*, 1675, Folger Shakespeare Library.	80
2.3	*Chi-Raq*, Dir. Lee, Amazon Studios, 2015.	83
3.1	*Watchmen*, Dir. Snyder, Warner Bros. Pictures, 2009.	88
3.2	*This Is Spinal Tap*, Dir. Reiner, Spinal Tap Productions, 1984.	89
4.1	*The Tempest*, Dir. Taymor, Touchstone Pictures, 2010.	129
5.1	"Hide and Q," *Star Trek: The Next Generation*, Dir. Bowle, Paramount, 1987.	148
5.2	"Emergence," *Star Trek: The Next Generation*, Dir. Bowle, Paramount, 1994.	155

Acknowledgments

We express our continued gratitude to Margaret W. Ferguson, our shared mentor, who has shaped so much of our understanding about the purchase of the early modern world on our own. We also thank other scholars who read portions of this book, asked pertinent questions, or helped us think through crucial issues as the project advanced. These individuals include Leah Allen, Tim Arner, Dustin Dixon, Ewan Fernie, Andrew Fleck, Katharine Goodland, Maurice Hunt, Sheiba Kaufman, Justin Kuhn, James Kuzner, Kathleen McDonald, Eric S. Mallin, Lawrence Manley, Angelo O. Mercado, Sonia Perello, Amy Woodbury Tease, Maggie Vinter, R.S. White, and Lea Williams. At Routledge, Polly Dodson and the anonymous readers helped us to think through how this book would speak to scholars of Shakespeare and scholars of Peace Studies. Routledge's Zoe Meyer was very helpful in bringing the typescript to book form. Nicole Polglaze provided invaluable support with finalizing the overall project. Sydnee Brown, Audrey Corcoran, Anna Emerson, and Elaine Thut were helpful readers in the final review of the typescript. Over the years, Vanessa Rapatz has provided ongoing friendship and support. We further thank Travis Morris and the Peace and War Center at Norwich University; the Peace and Conflict Studies Program at Grinnell College; the Departments of English at Grinnell College and Norwich University; and the staff of the Photography and Digital Imaging Department at the Folger Shakespeare Library.

Portions of the introduction and the first chapter were published in different form as "What's So Funny 'Bout, Peace, Love, and Shakespeare?: A Peace Studies Approach to *As You Like It*" in the journal *Shakespeare* (November 2016), reproduced by permission of Routledge Press. An earlier version of Chapter Three appeared in *Explorations in Renaissance Culture* 44.2 (2018), reproduced by permission of Brill. We are grateful to the anonymous readers at these journals for their thoughtful comments.

Introduction

The tide of war is receding

On a Friday evening in June 2017, Laura Loomer decided she had had enough of Shakespeare, or at least, she had had enough of this particular Shakespeare. During a production of *Julius Caesar* in Central Park, she stormed the stage and interrupted the assassination that we all knew was coming. Her remarks gained widespread attention and stirred seemingly endless debate about theater, politics, and the role of violence in both. This Caesar, after all, looked unmistakably like the newly elected President Trump, complete with blond hair, modern suit, and long red tie. As the production stopped with Brutus ready to kill, Loomer shouted to the audience, "Stop the normalization of political violence against the right! This is unacceptable!"[1] She was joined a few minutes later by another protestor, Jack Posobiec, who went so far as to compare everyone involved to Nazis. Nobody could deny that Shakespeare had been made blatantly and disturbingly political. This play about tyranny and civil war spoke directly to American audiences still grappling with the enormous implications of Trump's election, and the visions of blood on the stage demanded reflection. Was Shakespeare advocating assassination? Or denouncing the impulses that lead to violence? Could *Julius Caesar* promote civil war?

The collision of national politics, Shakespeare, and violence was clear. One can say that this has always been the case with *Julius Caesar*. The play contains an idiom repeated so often that it's easy to forget it's actually Shakespeare: "Cry 'havoc!' and let slip the dogs of war" (3.1.276). In that line, Antony announces aggression without restraint, as if violence had reached the point of inevitability. In the summer of 2017, it seemed all too relevant. Shakespeare and American politics unmistakably collided, and many feared the "dogs of war" would only get more vicious with time.

This book will ask questions about Shakespeare, war, and peace. We hope to see not just what the plays and poetry suggest about questions of violence, but how those same plays and poems can help us to understand better our own attitudes toward narratives that depict the inter-relationship between violence and non-violence. We hope to shine a light on Shakespeare's pacifism as much as to shine a light on our own patterns of thought. We are writing at a particularly crucial moment in American politics. In his first months in the office, President Trump has demonstrated his dedication to violence in the name of politics. Beyond the hope to "bomb the shit out of" terrorists, Trump has announced his intent to bolster American military spending by $54 billion.[2] He claims that he wants to rebuild a depleted force, to restore strength to what had grown weak. In April 2017, he authorized the military to drop the "Mother of All Bombs" in Afghanistan.[3] In August, he threatened North Korea with "fire and fury, and frankly power the likes of which the world has never seen before."[4] Dogs of war indeed.

But what are the origins of Trump's belligerence? And what are its ends? What would Shakespeare have said about it all? We look to uncover attitudes toward peace in the 21st century, knowing that Caesar's death somehow looms equally in the ancient past, in Shakespeare's re-staging, and in Central

Park in 2017. The case of *Julius Caesar* suggests that Shakespeare thought a great deal about the causes of war. But we want to pursue another option – that Shakespeare has a great deal more to say about the causes of peace. That he was a pacifist still worth hearing. To begin, we look back to 2009.

Obama understood that it was a strange moment when he accepted the Nobel Peace Prize in 2009. Despite his promises of de-escalation or reconciliation, this president was still at war in at least two places. We now know that over the next several years Obama would still face drone warfare, renewed terror, and vicious violence. The contradiction of him receiving a peace prize is clear, but at the moment, the award implied that things were changing. Peace had come, with the obvious exception of the ongoing wars. All Obama had to do was explain the paradox. All he had to do was reconcile decades of thinking that simultaneously denounces war while also defending war.

Did he succeed? Not quite, and what did come out reveals contemporary confusion on issues of peace and war.

Obama began his acceptance speech with his trademark language of hope. This award, he said, "speaks to our highest aspirations – that for all the cruelty and hardship of our world, we are not mere prisoners of fate. Our actions matter, and can bend history in the direction of justice."[5] In that opening, he admits the possibility for change, and he suggests that "we" can make conscious choices and manage our "actions" to bring about that change. Even though "our world" – understood here as the real world free of naivety – offers nothing but cruelty, history doesn't have to be that way. At least, that's Obama's first sentence. Trump's escalation of war puts a bitter period on the thought, yet the inconsistencies were already there, just below the surface.

Just as soon as he gets to the next paragraph, Obama's tone shifts and the speech openly admits the moment's contradictions. He says, "And yet I would be remiss if I did not acknowledge the considerable controversy" of awarding him the Nobel Peace Prize. He goes on:

> But perhaps the most profound issue surrounding my receipt of this prize is the fact that I am the Commander-in-Chief of the military of a nation in the midst of two wars. One of these wars is winding down. The other is a conflict that America did not seek; one in which we are joined by 42 other countries – including Norway – in an effort to defend ourselves and all nations from further attacks.

If the first part of the speech strikes an optimistic mood, defeatism intrudes here. American military action in the Middle East persisted even as Obama accepted the prize, implying that this peace prize was always more about the future than the present. In fact, the speech explicitly calls out the awkward fit among the award, the moment at which it was given, and the person to whom it was awarded. Obama insists that the war in Afghanistan was one "that America did not seek," but it's also one supported by an international coalition. Already, he justifies the continued war, one that would go on to become America's longest. The costs are necessary because they constitute the wartime "effort" to achieve safety. Obama attacks so that he can protect "all nations from further attacks." The only other choice, it seems, would be to make no effort at all, and so to fuel violence.

The confusions and ambiguities don't stop there. "War, in one form or another, appeared with the first man," he says. "At the dawn of history, its morality was not questioned; it was simply a fact, like drought or disease – the manner in which tribes and then civilizations sought power and settled their differences." Obama started with hope and the notion that "we can bend history" to achieve peaceful resolutions. Now, he adopts the language of practicality and inevitability. Throughout human existence, we are told, conflict was "simply a fact," as unavoidable as the weather, and this speech on the subject of peace has morphed into a defense of war. Obama wrestles with his subject, at once acknowledging the importance of peace work and simultaneously conceding that he will be bound to violence. He explains, for instance, the concept of Augustine's "just war," a defense of military violence that demands certain conditions be met: "if [war] is waged as a last resort or in self-defense; if the force used is proportional; and if, whenever possible, civilians are spared from violence." Not that Obama uses the "just war" theory to defend all military interventions, just those conducted by the United States and its allies:

> Of course, we know that for most of history, this concept of "just war" was rarely observed. The capacity of human beings to think up new ways to kill one another proved inexhaustible, as did our capacity to exempt from mercy those who look different or pray to a different God. Wars between armies gave ways to wars between nations – total wars in which the distinction between combatant and civilian became blurred. In the span of 30 years, such carnage would twice engulf this continent. And while it's hard to conceive of a cause more just than the defeat of the Third Reich and the Axis powers, World War II was a conflict in which the total number of civilians who died exceeded the number of soldiers who perished.

Those terrible losses cannot be ignored, and World War II is a tragedy – not just for those who fought, but for all civilians who suffered or died over its course. Technically, it does not meet the conditions for a "just war" simply because civilians were not spared. But Obama cannot go so far as to say it wasn't a "just war."

The narrative of World War II drives Obama's theory throughout the speech: Always avoid war, except when the narrative is just and you must use violence. Indeed, that very narrative has dominated popular impressions of war in America. As General Tony Zinni puts it, "Our World War II experience became the model for how we organized our military forces. It became the model for how we expected conflicts to unfold. It became the model for major combat operations. It became the model for how we looked at enemies."[6] A model "for how we expected conflicts to unfold" isn't just a matter of military strategy; it's a matter of point-of-view, storytelling, and plotting. Obama invokes that same narrative in his acceptance of the peace prize. If the narrative of warfare is "just," then peace can be imagined as an ultimate goal. The same narrative will be used as the model for understanding all American conflict, even the "War on Terror." That means Obama can ask his audience to "think in new ways about the notions of just war and the imperatives of a just peace" with sincerity, while also defending the old ways of militarism and organized conflict. The narrative is already written, imagined as new while also repeating the ideas and violent tragedies of the past. History no longer bends to our will; we face evil as it is, recognizing that war is necessary and inevitable.

The speech, then, is strangely perplexing and often confounding. It calls for innovation and creativity while simultaneously calling for realism and pragmatism. At one point,

Obama says, "I know there's nothing weak – nothing passive – nothing naïve – in the creed and lives of Gandhi and King." He admits that peace work involves deliberate non-action, especially if perceptions of violence are to change. But no sooner does Obama make that concession than he turns to the opposite point, "We must begin by acknowledging the hard truth: We will not eradicate violent conflict in our lifetimes. There will be times when nations – acting individually or in concert – will find the use of force not only necessary but morally justified." The hard truth remains, undermining the peace work of the very organization granting Obama the award. To ignore that "hard truth," one assumes, is to give over to idealism, fantasy, and passivity – the very notions that interest Shakespeare. Obama insists, "I face the world as it is, and cannot stand idle in the face of threats to the American people." War will go on. Otherwise, idleness takes over. And narratives, we presume, get nowhere in idleness. They require active participants, engaging in struggle, facing the hard truths with soberness and willingness to fight.

When Obama withdrew troops from Iraq in 2011, he proclaimed that "the tide of war is receding."[7] Troops were returning home, and the conflict was pronounced over. "After nearly nine years," he said, "America's war in Iraq will be over." Obama uses the future tense throughout, constructing a vision of a new and different time to be.

Except we know that potential wasn't quite fulfilled. War went on. Troops returned to Iraq. America went back to its narratives of necessary action, justified war, and hard truths. Retrospect, it would seem, shows us the inevitability of war. The world just gets in the way, and the same plots are recycled. Andrew J. Bacevich nicely articulates one of the central questions that drives our study, phrasing it in terms of a *Pax*

Americana following the Vietnam War that has since given way to protracted – and unwanted – war. He writes,

> How exactly did the end of the Long Peace so quickly yield the Long War? Seeing themselves as a peaceful people, Americans remain wedded to the conviction that the conflicts in which they find themselves embroiled are not of their own making. The global war on terror is no exception. Certain of our own benign intentions, we reflexively assign responsibility for war to others, typically malignant Hitler-like figures inexplicably bent on denying us the peace that is our fondest wish.[8]

Bacevich is reading the same plots, grounded in the "malignant Hitler-like figures" that dominate public imaginations. But what are the alternatives? Could a different plot open up the possibilities for peace?

With that, let's turn to somebody who knew a thing or two about plots. Shakespeare, far from "normalizing" violence, might just offer a way out.

IN LOVE WITH WAR

Shakespeare understood narratives – how they work, what audiences expect, why audiences crave conflict, and how to engineer a resolution. Centuries of performances and adaptations speak to his dramatic insight. We follow that suggestion with a more unusual argument: Because Shakespeare understood narratives, he understood peace. For that reason, his literary insights possess an unrecognized value today. As a dramatist, he clearly has less at stake than the president of a superpower in the 21st century. Shakespeare obviously couldn't foresee today's military conflicts, let alone drone warfare or the "Mother of All Bombs." What he did understand were the narratives and languages of reconciliation. As Sarah Beckwith puts it, "in Shakespeare's writing is an extraordinary, unprecedented expansion in the expressive range, precision, and flexibility of language as it takes up this terrible burden and gift of human relating when nothing but language secures or grounds human relations."[9] He offers the grammar of forgiveness (a phrase Beckwith uses to name her study of Shakespeare's plays), knowing that "*human* speech [. . .] makes or breaks the bonds between people."[10] By looking at how he envisioned peace, we can begin to see our own blind spots. We can begin to learn the assumptions that put violent bloodshed at the forefront of imagination and treat war as the inevitable result of the world's hard facts. We can understand Shakespeare as a participant in Peace Studies, no matter if he preceded this field of study by about 350 years.[11]

To treat Shakespeare as a proponent for peace has not always been the typical approach. For many Shakespeareans, war never ends, and so the conversation revolves around war. *Henry V* may give thanks to God for a decisive victory at Agincourt; he may also swear his devotion to the "surety of our leagues" with France (5.2.344). Audiences and readers, though, understand that these fragile resolutions must fail. Shakespeare already told us so in the *Henry VI* plays, when war wearily resumes. Graham Holderness sums up the effect in his description of *Henry IV Part 1*: "it is war that now constitutes the inescapable condition of existence for the state of England [. . .] Conflict cannot be prevented or cured; it can only be suppressed."[12] For many historians, those same lines would seem to describe the Elizabethan age just as well. Curtis C. Breight, for instance, describes Elizabeth's regime as a "State of Terror," responsible for "thousands of slaughtered

Catholics, hundreds of thousands of disposable soldiers, sailors, and members of their families, and countless other casualties."[13] The people of Shakespeare's age lived in times of rebellion, invasion, and state-sponsored terrorism. It would seem no wonder that war turned into the "inescapable condition" for one of the era's star playwrights.

Shakespeareans follow suit in stressing his depictions of war. Certainly, there has been no lack of research regarding the place of military conflict in Shakespeare's canon. These scholars have analyzed the functions, dynamics, and outcomes of battle. They have asked whether Shakespeare celebrates military heroism and the ability of war to inspire the "band of brothers." They have examined how Shakespeare adapts the historical materials of his period. And they have asked whether Shakespeare actually denounces war by depicting its horrors and injustices. As Edmund King puts it, "recent scholarly work has taken for granted the centrality of Shakespeare to the cultural side of conflict."[14] Even when peace comes up, it always returns to the "hard truth" of war, just as Obama couldn't keep from defending the use of violence. Yet, we can resist this point-of-view that insists on inevitability. Laurence Lerner, for instance, makes a plea for Peace Studies as a necessary — in fact, an overdue — school of literary criticism, committed to showing that "war is an evil which we are trying to learn how to eradicate."[15] His first case study is (not surprisingly) *Henry V*. Following well-established lines of criticism, Lerner searches out "moments when the text complicates the simple heroism which it appears to glorify" and "those occasions when we resist the text."[16] In either case, though, Lerner starts with scenes of violent belligerence. Peace is imagined as its negative, the counterpoint to war's destruction. Paola Pugliatti similarly accepts the primacy and unavoidability of conflict even as she explores Shakespeare's resistance to militarism and violence. War "justly waged," she concludes, "is the prerequisite of peace."[17] While she reveals Shakespeare's skepticism toward the "just war," her approach accepts a quite narrow definition of peace. A much more expanded definition would treat peace neither as the end of war nor as the conclusion of things. The narrow conception imagines peace as a negative condition, as the state of not doing things and as simply recovering until the next period of conflict. Fortunately, Peace Studies gives us another view.

Cynical critics could easily rehearse the notion that peace is an ending and so dismiss "Peace Studies" as the study of nothing. Johan Galtung, however, insisted in his foundational statements in 1964 that the field was a viable one, just as worthy of examination as war. In an opening editorial for the *Journal of Peace Research*, he broadened the scope of things by building on the distinctions between negative peace and positive peace; in doing so, he pioneered the discipline itself. Negative peace implies "the absence of violence, the absence of war" – that is, it looks at the conclusions of conflict.[18] Positive peace expands in the other direction, proclaiming that "peace" extends to all dimensions of society, even when that society is not at war. It turns the pursuit of peace from "let's end war" to "let's generate peace." In that reframing, peacebuilding emerges as an active and dynamic process, never idle and never ending. What Galtung asks, then, is that we think not of eliminating war, but rather of generating peace. And when peace is made a positive action, it can also develop into a plot of its own.

In his later work, Galtung expands upon the theoretical bases of such peacebuilding. "Peace is what we have when creative conflict transformation takes place nonviolently,"[19] he writes. It's important to recognize that for Galtung, conflict never disappears entirely, and to hope so leads to inevitable charges of naïveté or idealism. Galtung goes on to name three separate branches of Peace Studies: empirical, critical, and constructive.[20] These branches respectively look to the past, the present, and the future. In looking at the past, researchers can test whether theories of peaceful resolution were borne out in specific historical circumstances. In studying the present, scholars can judge whether contemporary practices meet with stated values, as in whether treatment of war prisoners matches what a group says should happen to prisoners. Constructivism – the branch looking at the future – proposes something potentially more radical. It "takes theories about what might work and brings them together with values about what ought to work."[21] Although Galtung concentrates on the social sciences, literature demands its own place in his framework. The imaginative texts – the plays, poems, and essays – of historical periods offer data of the past, but they simultaneously provide imaginative accounts of future possibilities. Through the work of fiction, a play can give an opportunity to envision the "creative conflict transformation" that Galtung urges. The impact for literary studies is significant: The literary text can serve as a constructivist study that takes facts of historical accounts and reimagines the possibilities for resolution. No longer a void, peace becomes dramatic and indeed full of conflict. Its ends, however, are nonviolent. So Shakespeare can write about peace while still drawing heroes, while still giving more than a stage clearing at the end of Henry V.

This book's approach to Shakespeare and peace, then, may feel anachronistic. We're taking concepts from contemporary social sciences and mapping them onto literature written in the 16th and 17th centuries. Indeed, we intend (in part) for that. We assume a "presentist" perspective, meaning that Shakespeare comes to us through the present and that we can see him only through the lens of our own concerns. According to Hugh Grady and Terence Hawkes, "the first duty of a credible presentist criticism must be to acknowledge that the questions we ask of any literary text will inevitably be shaped by our own concerns."[22] In fact, Grady and Hawkes argue that approaching the past with an awareness of our own moment just might be "the basis of the only effective purchase on Shakespeare that we're able to make."[23] To that bold stance, we bring the insights of Madhavi Menon, who goes beyond the claims of presentism to insist upon the "unhistorical Shakespeare." Her focus on sexuality and desire leads Menon to a startling conclusion, that assuming "chronological difference as the basis for sound historical knowledge" leads to limited — indeed, homophobic — understandings of history.[24] In other words, we shouldn't simply assume the past and present are invariably different. Menon therefore embraces sameness and sees the present not as separate from the past, but in some ways informing it. She writes, "there is no method for reconstructing the past that is not anachronistic."[25] We assert Shakespeare is a scholar of Peace Studies, knowing that we indulge the anachronism. That approach lets us see not just what Shakespeare can show us about peace but what peace can illuminate in Shakespeare. We can't come to the literature without seeing the present in the past and the past in the present.

In the 2011 film of Shakespeare's *Coriolanus*, Ralph Fiennes assumes the same. The play takes place in ancient Rome, where a triumphant general fends off invading armies and callously dismisses the pleas of the common people. In that plot, Ralph Fiennes finds compelling commentary on 21st-century war. He dresses his soldiers in today's military uniforms and gives them today's military technology – that is, when they don't grapple in the mud with knives and broken glass in the savage attempt to gut one another. He also shot the film in Serbia, in locations that confront audiences with the costs of war. The damage is visible in the facades of buildings, peppered with bullet holes and the lasting scars of conflict. Fiennes cites that "grittiness" as a reason for shooting in Serbia. Then he names the main setting of his play "a place calling itself Rome," drawing the moniker from a 1970s stage adaptation of Shakespeare's play by John Osborne. His Rome is not exactly Rome. It's a contemporary Rome that could be, a Rome that has fallen to the precarity of today's times. The "bruised battered quality of some of the locations" speaks to the concerns of *Coriolanus* – primarily its despairing view of our deep desire for prolonged violence.[26] His film makes clear the enormous costs that come when positive peace is ignored or outright denied. It reveals the gaps in Obama's logic – that which associates peace with "idleness" and fails to conceive of a story without bloodshed. Coriolanus desperately needs to learn about positive peace.

That the film appeared in 2011 makes for a profound coincidence. Obama announced that "the tide of war is receding" at the same time a film lamented that the tide hasn't budged at all. In fact, *Coriolanus* grimly suggests that maybe we lack the ability to even conceive of such an end, and that we wouldn't want that end even if it did come. In the opening scenes, Coriolanus – named Martius until he earns the title of Coriolanus in the second act – denounces a rebellion of citizens who demand food. In Shakespeare's play, senators ask these plebeians directly to stop the violence; in Fiennes' film, these senators speak behind the safety of TV cameras. Only Coriolanus faces them, and his wrath is palpable. He scowls:

> What would you have, you curs
> That like nor peace nor war? The one affrights you,
> The other makes you proud. He that trusts to you,
> Where he should find lions, finds you hares,
> Where foxes, geese.
>
> (1.1.157–161)

In Coriolanus' mind, these civilians deserve neither conflict nor harmony. During a war, they are perfectly happy to let Coriolanus get his hands bloody. In peacetime, the people grow resentful and so rebel against those same aristocrats. One can never know what the people will become. Coriolanus' scarred face testifies to the battle hardened cynicism that he projects upon his subjects. The warrior remains stable, and he finds "peace" only in bloodshed. Without it, the people grow restless, rebellious, and violent. Peace, Coriolanus seems to suggest, is just a dream. He, of course, faces the "hard facts" of ceaseless conflict in the world, just as Obama takes his peace prize while acknowledging ongoing war.

When this Roman hero ventures abroad to fight with his long-standing enemy Aufidius, he thrives in the action, as if it were the only thing to give him purpose or meaning. The fight takes him to the city of Corioles. As Coriolanus approaches the stronghold of Aufidius, Fiennes makes clear the parallels to modern warfare. A series of IEDs laced under the city explode, pushing the Romans back. The scene then cuts back to Rome, to Coriolanus' worrying wife, Virgilia, who watches as Coriolanus' son practices shooting with a BB gun. This boy has already learned the lessons of warfare, and no wonder. Coriolanus' mother assures Virgilia that violence is always the right choice: "If my son were my husband, I should freelier rejoice in that absence wherein he won honour than in the embracements of his bed where he would show most love" (1.3.2–4). Fiennes here departs from Shakespeare, crosscutting between this speech and images of the ongoing battle. The effect is at once troubling and profound. Volumnia – Coriolanus' mother – reverses a well-known 1960s peace slogan when she essentially says to her daughter-in-law: *Better to make war, not love*. The action that matters takes place in the battlefield. Volumnia then slips into a fantasy of warfare. She says, "Methinks I hear your husband's drum, [. . .] Methinks I see him stamp thus, and call thus:/'Come on, you cowards, you were got in fear/Though you were born in Rome'" (1.3.26–31). The lines create a sound bridge to Coriolanus cajoling his troops to continued fighting. Her vision becomes the very stuff of war.

In a dreamlike haze caused by explosions back on the battlefield, Coriolanus addresses the camera directly. He threatens his men and audience alike: "Mend and charge home,/ Or by the fires of heaven I'll leave the foe/And make my wars on you" (1.5.9–11). His aggression targets everyone. Aufidius may be the sworn enemy driving this particular attack, but Coriolanus will not hesitate to turn his aggression outward, directing it to his own troops, his own city, even his own audience. When the two soldiers finally do meet, their battle becomes intensely personal. Aufidius and Coriolanus fight with knives first, eschewing the modern guns, and they touch foreheads in a gesture both vicious and intimate (Figure I.1). If Volumnia imagines that the battlefield is better than

Figure I.1 Making a connection (*Coriolanus*, Dir. Fiennes, Icon Entertainment International and BBC Films, 2011)

the bed, Coriolanus seems to agree. The two soldiers crash through a window, land in the street, and soon embrace as they try to kill each other. Aufidius grabs a piece of rubble and tries to bludgeon his enemy; he uses the wreckage of war to enact more war. And the affectionate relationship blends into the bellicose, as if the impulse for bloodshed were driven by desire, attraction, and passion.[27] Perhaps we shouldn't be surprised when Coriolanus turns to the camera and threatens us. In Fiennes' film, it's what we all want.

The style of the war film, that is, suggests something profound about military conflict: that the desire for war always comes first, before the justification for war. In his Nobel Prize speech, Obama gets the causal arrow wrong. He assumes that the American ideals of freedom and justice will demand that soldiers take up arms when those ideals are threatened. Fiennes' revision exposes what's already in Shakespeare's play. The bloody action drives the principled stand, not the other way around. Coriolanus wants to fight. He'll find the reasons to fight later. Obama struggles with the desire for peace against the realities of war because he fails to admit what Coriolanus knows: that the war itself creates the reason for going to war. The reasons, as counter-intuitive as it might be, do not generate the war.

To make this plain in his film, Fiennes fills *Coriolanus* with TV screens that give necessary exposition. A series of talking heads act as a Greek chorus and explain the movement of troops, popular unrest, and the violent triumphs of Coriolanus. We can just treat this as a simple device: Fiennes needs characters to give information, and the faux-CNN coverage is the fastest way. But the movie's sidelong glance at the desire for war suggests the possibility that the talking heads are creating the desire for more war. The coverage feeds that desire for excitement and intimacy that in *Coriolanus* imaginatively replaces sex. Without war, after all, what would these news anchors talk about? And when it comes to Shakespeare's play, we can ask the same. Without war, what can this play do?

If narrative depends upon conflict, then how could peace – with all of its resolutions and conclusions – ever inspire riveting theater? For too many Shakespeareans, that has too often been the implicit assumption, whether they see it or not. As J. G. Russell quips, "War is an activity; peace is a state or condition."[28] So peace, he concludes, "has no heroes."[29] With that line in mind, the anti-war movement has failed before it even began, undone by the very need for a plot. That devastating critique also reinforces the idea that peace is lazy, boring, and effeminate. In his review of the criticism on Shakespeare and war, Andrew Hiscock argues that "peacetime in plays such as *Richard III* or *Troilus and Cressida* comes to signify cultural disorientation and moral vacancy."[30] Hiscock supports that summation with early modern statements on the vacuous dangers of peace, including Barnabe Rich's *Opinion Deified* (1613). In that text, peace forces men to "become *Hermophrodites*, halfe-men, halfe-harlots, it effeminates their minds."[31] War creates heroes;

peace creates "half-men." Volumnia, of course, would agree. Time spent at home means time spent in a negative void, without merit and without masculinity. War means something is happening, something to be reported on TV, something to be celebrated. Peace? That's just the time before the next encounter between Coriolanus and Aufidius.

In a line that Fiennes cuts from his *Coriolanus*, Shakespeare interrogates that same idea. At this point in the play, things have turned for Coriolanus. When he refuses to appease the common people, the war hero is driven from Rome. His humiliation is public and total. Coriolanus travels to Antium, where he joins with Aufidius. This Roman would rather collaborate with his sworn enemy in the ruin of Rome than admit political defeat. When he enters the city of Antium – where Aufidius is now living – two comic serving men comment that the city had been growing bored in its easy harmony. "This peace is nothing but to rust iron, increase tailors, and breed ballad-makers" (4.5.216–217), says one servant. The other responds in kind: "Let me have war, say I. [...] Peace is a very apoplexy, lethargy; mulled, deaf, sleepy, insensible; a getter of more bastard children than war's a destroyer of men" (4.5.218–222). Until the battle commences, nothing happens. The "ballad-makers" will write terrible songs for lack of anything better to do. Peace itself is "lethargy" – laziness and idleness that actually create more problems than war. As the first serving man says, peace "makes men hate one another" (4.5.226). War, we can assume, brings them together and gives them something to do.

The tragedy in *Coriolanus* suitably comes when a treaty is drawn up. In this contradictory world, peace accords won't stop violence; rather, they just inspire more bloodshed. In a pivotal scene, Coriolanus is dissuaded from destroying his own city by his mother, and the film conspicuously shows the "Peace Treaty" being signed immediately after. We can see "Peace" emblazoned clearly, signaling that events are drawing to a close. After making the accords, Coriolanus returns to the Volsces and a simmering Aufidius. "We have made peace/ With no less honour to the Antiates/Than same to th' Romans" (5.6.79–81), Coriolanus says. Aufidius is quick to denounce his former partner as a "traitor" (5.6.85). With war over, the personal feud can erupt. After all, neither soldier could admit the "lethargy" of a true peace. They must begin another bitter fight or else give themselves over to idleness, boredom, and uselessness. In the film, Coriolanus dies as Aufidius plunges a knife into the body, holding his partner in a bitter hug. It's fitting. This renewed war allows one to kill the other in a twisted display of affection. This is the damning view of Fiennes' film: Shakespeare denounces not war, but instead the emotional and psychological needs to fight wars. The tragedy of *Coriolanus* comes from that paradox – only war will bring people together. Then, they can kill each other with love.

Both the film and the play, finally, speak to the very concerns Galtung articulates in his foundational statements for Peace Studies. War goes on because these characters think of war as activity. Peace is an ending and therefore amounts to annihilation. Shakespeare's play – like President Obama's speech – says, "I cannot stand idle." So we are left with a tragedy in which the only meaningful action requires self-destruction. It means searching out the new war until it kills you.

We quote again from Andrew Bacevich. In an analysis from 2005, Bacevich used a provocative subtitle: "How Americans Are Seduced by War." That language of love and sexual attraction is a coincidence, but a telling one nonetheless. The film version of *Coriolanus* characterizes the 21st-century Western forces as falling in love with war. In Fiennes' film, it's the only feeling worth having. Bacevich makes his own damnations clear:

> To state the matter bluntly, Americans in our own time have fallen prey to militarism, manifesting itself in a romanticized view of soldiers, a tendency to see military power as the truest measure of national greatness, and outsized expectations regarding the efficacy of force. To a degree without precedent in U.S. history, Americans have come to define the nation's strength and well-being in terms of military preparedness, military action, and the fostering of (or nostalgia for) military ideas.[32]

Getting some action comes to mean military action, and there seems no way out.

PEACE SPEAKS

Did Shakespeare know any alternative in the late 16th century? Could he have imagined a different course of history, away from war and toward nonviolent resolution? To those questions, one could certainly mumble a cynical "no" and imagine the past as one of endless conflict. We have already seen Obama admit just that view when he says, "War, in one form or another, appeared with the first man." Standing with a peace prize in one hand, Obama here gives the argument that violent conflict is inevitable. History confirms just that — it tells a story of endless bloodshed, from day one until now. We may associate Shakespeare's day with all of its Elizabethan "golden age" trappings, but it is ultimately no different. We have also seen already how historians have repeated this supposed truism; we in fact can find its relatives in the early modern period. It's an easy narrative to buy, but that doesn't mean it has to be the only one.

Niccolò Machiavelli's *The Prince* (1532) gives a succinct version of the "practical" argument. This book serves as a guide to realpolitik, to admitting the necessary realities of political rule without the blindness of moral ideologies getting in the way. And Machiavelli makes himself clear when it comes to the subject of war: "A prince [. . .] should have no other object, no other thought, no other subject of study, than war."[33] All choices lead to violence in the world of *The Prince*; therefore, any savvy leader should be ready at all times for that violence. Peace is an illusion, for conflict is always on its way. Machiavelli writes, "It is clear that when princes have thought more about the refinements of life than about war, they have lost their positions. The quickest way to lose a state is to neglect this art."[34] That view rests in the notion that humanity will always fight, and if leaders must choose between the peaceful or violent way, those ready for battle will inevitably come out on top. Best to always study war. Writing in 1513, Machiavelli seems to have anticipated the ideas of *Coriolanus*, that peace equates to laziness and weakness. A prince, says Machiavelli, "must never idle away his days of peace, but vigorously make capital that will pay off in times of adversity; thus, when fortune changes, it will find him in a position to resist."[35] Coriolanus would appreciate such advice, and he might even suggest that any realist should agree. Never mind that his own, or his mother's, fantasies of warfare cloud the notion of realpolitik with their own fevered dreams.

That vision of world affairs speaks to a simplistic view of the world. It's an easy narrative to tell, but that doesn't mean it's the only one.

Shakespeare's period also saw its own version of peace proponents, those who countered Machiavelli's cynical language with pleas for understanding and mutual cooperation. In fact, when Henry VIII came to the throne in 1509, some in his court applauded the rise of a true scholar who could bring morality to the throne. Robert P. Adams describes this atmosphere in his history of humanism of the 16th century. As he shows, the group of scholars at the center of this movement – John Colet, Thomas More, and Desiderius Erasmus – put their faith in learning and scholarly exchange, driving in turn a carefully considered rejection of war.[36]

Such an ideal would have appealed to Erasmus. In 1508, he composed the first of a few essays on the subject, "Dulce bellum inexpertis" – or "War is sweet for those who have not tried it." He makes the thesis strikingly clear. "If there is any human activity that should be approached with caution," he writes, "that activity is war, for there is nothing more wicked, more disastrous, more widely destructive, more persistently ingrained, more hateful, more unworthy in every respect of a man, not to say a Christian."[37] His predecessor Augustine had made the case for a just war in the 5th century, the theory that Obama struggles with in the 21st. Erasmus wouldn't have it and was said to have repeated a line from Cicero: "The most unjust peace is preferable to the most just war."[38] Even though the bellicose may defend war by assuming its inevitability, such a line is "unworthy" to any Christian, let alone any human being.

So Erasmus retells his history of mankind and explicitly rejects the notions of inherent violence. War, in this view, does not begin with the first man, but with those who corrupted a naturally benevolent mankind. He asks,

> If we consider just the condition and appearance of the
> human body, is it not apparent at once that Nature, or rather
> God, created this animal not for war but for friendship, not
> for destruction but for preservation, not for aggression but
> to be helpful?[39]

No claws, tusks, or horns. Not even natural protection like a shell or hide, just the fragile and vulnerable human skin. Obviously, if violence were an inborn condition, nature would give man some means of inflicting that violence. Instead, Erasmus concludes that humankind is born into passivity and so must dedicate itself to collaboration and good will. He goes on, "Not content with these gifts Nature gave to man alone the use of speech and reason, the thing that is able above all else to create and nourish good will, so that nothing should be managed among men by force."[40] Erasmus concludes the portrait with a religious argument – God imparts to humanity a divine nature such that they take natural pleasure in helping one another.

War perverts the image of a gracious and vulnerable creature. Erasmus imagines Nature looking out at the battlefields, at weapons fashioned to kill another being not just one by one, but in untold numbers, for reasons that only compound previous battles. The fight is going on because the fight is going on. Erasmus then puts words into Nature's mouth: "There was one creature I brought forth made entirely for kindly actions – peaceful, friendly, helpful. What has happened to make him degenerate into a beast like this? I recognize nothing in him of the man I created. What evil genius has degraded my work?"[41] For Erasmus, it's anything but natural. War did not start with the first man. Nor is peace some sort of delusion. Peace and cooperation are natural – something that Coriolanus fundamentally does not understand.

Erasmus didn't stop there. He continues the argument in a second essay titled "A Complaint of Peace Spurned and Rejected by the Whole World," first written in 1517. Here, Erasmus synthesizes and reiterates points he makes in earlier writing, putting it all under the umbrella of an evocative first sentence that was added in the 1529 edition: "Peace speaks."[42] Peace now takes the podium, making herself heard and understood as not just the absence of war but an active presence begging for recognition. Indeed, Peace says that she could very well leave mankind since they have no use for pacifism, but she feels pity and so makes the effort to bring some sanity and reason to the madness of war. The state of the world, then, compels her to do something, to answer all of the flimsy justifications for war. She will take on the logic of Coriolanus and Obama in order to show that there are always alternatives to war.

Among the defenses of war comes one suspiciously close to that which Obama offered in 2009: that war is born of compulsion. No one chooses to go to war; they are forced to do so, made to do so by the course of human nature and the path of history. On that point, Peace rolls her eyes and soundly rejects such logic:

> But I have long been hearing the sort of excuse clever men produce their own wrongdoing. They protest that they act under compulsion and are dragged unwillingly into war. Pull off your mask, drop your pretenses, examine your own heart, and you will find that anger, ambition, and folly brought you to war, not any constraint – unless you define constraint as

something not altogether to your liking! Such trappings are for the people; God is not to be fooled by pretense.[43]

When one assumes that war will always happen, then any event gives the necessary excuse. In *Why Nations Fight*, Richard Ned Lebow revisits the question of what causes war. In the face of those who would claim security or "the real world" as the underlying motivation, Lebow cites less practical reasons. In his study, wars follow from the desire for national prestige and revenge, motivations not nearly as noble as some would pretend. In fact, Lebow finds national standing as the cause of 58% of wars since 1648.[44] Erasmus here nods his head. Claims of security or practicality are merely masks and pretenses, the latest in the perversions that allows rulers – or characters like Coriolanus – to get around the clear demands for peace. These same princes may shout to God, "Grant us peace, we beseech you, hear us!," but God has already given them their answer: "Why do you mock me? You are asking me to remove what you bring on yourselves by your own choice. You pray to be let off what is your own responsibility."[45] So much for the reality of the world forcing war upon hapless, peace-loving humanity. In this account, they bring war upon themselves and then have the gall to suggest they didn't want it. Peace goes on to offer an analogy to the domestic relationship, an analogy Shakespeare will address in his own ways. She says, "If any affront can start a war – why, who has nothing to complain of? Incidents arise between husband and wife which are best overlooked, unless you want their mutual good will to be destroyed. If something of the same sort arises between princes, why need there be an immediate rush to arms?"[46] Other possibilities for resolution remain. Assuming violence is the only outcome leads – not surprisingly – to more violence. Better to look for an alternative, for the creative conflict resolution advocated by Peace Studies.

If Machiavelli gives the "realist" position to the new prince, it is worth noting that Erasmus did give his own manual of instruction for rulers. He wrote *The Education of a Christian Prince* in 1516, in the midst of his other writings on peace, and just three years after *The Prince* first showed up in manuscript form. Although Erasmus does not specifically respond to Machiavelli, he tackles the same problems: How best to help the ruler lead successfully? In *The Education of a Christian Prince*, the teacher must lead the prince down the path of moral education, not the practical brutalities of Machiavelli's guidebook. This education of course leads to peacefulness. Erasmus' ideal ruler avoids war at all costs and commits to the universal peace. He writes, "Although ancient writers divided the whole theory of statecraft into two sets of skills, those of peace and of war, our first and foremost concern must be for training the prince in the skills relevant to wise administration in time of peace, because with them he must strive to his utmost for this end: that the devices of war may never be needed."[47] Even when the "watch-dog" is in power, the task remains the same – preserve peace. This goal stands out first and foremost. Machiavelli's prince prepares for war because that is the default state of things. Erasmus' prince prepares for peace, the natural state of mankind and the only worthwhile condition.

War fosters more war, but that should never be considered the only choice for the ruler. Erasmus insists again and again on the moral and practical faults. He writes,

> The truly Christian prince [. . .] should then consider how desirable, how honorable, how wholesome a thing is peace;

> on the other hand, how calamitous as well as wicked a thing
> is war, and how even the most just of wars brings with it a
> train of evils – if indeed any war can really be called just.[48]

That instruction follows from his philosophical treatises on peace, and Erasmus works to shift definitions of honor and idleness from their limitations. The legendary heroes of classical literature are hardly heroic when they only sought out the corrupt praises that come with violence. Their reputations amount to yet further deception. Erasmus argues, "When you hear of Achilles, Xerxes, Cyrus, Darius, or Julius, do not be at all overwhelmed by the enormous prestige of their names; you are hearing about great raging bandits, for that is what Seneca calls them several times."[49] The true prince must reject such role models and rethink what it means to be at peace, and what it means to be idle. We'll show in this book alternate heroes who embrace idleness – not Achilles or Coriolanus, but the lovers and jokesters who will happily find the worthwhileness in doing nothing.

Erasmus gives over a section of his book to the prince's activities in peacetime, suggesting that the absence of war is hardly a time of inaction. During this time, rulers should attend to their people as farmers tend to their crops or doctors treat their patients. The Christian prince should "imitate the worthy Scipio, who used to say that he was never less alone than when he was on his own and never less idle than when he had time to spare."[50] During times of peace, then, the wise rulers find themselves most busy, for that is the time of education, public works, and continual improvement. Where *Coriolanus* treats peace as an apoplexy, Erasmus sees it as a period of activity and engagement. Persian kings, Erasmus says, went about it the wrong way: "They used to fitter away the rest of their time in games or mad military adventures, as if the noble prince had nothing to do in time of peace, when in fact a whole crop of good works lies open to him, if only he thinks like a prince."[51] War, then, is a distraction, a dangerous way to fill up empty hours. Those who need it simply cannot conceive of the learning and advances that would take care of this supposed "idleness."

And the soldiers who partake in war? They can hardly be called more active or less idle than the busy scholar who thrives in peacetime. Certainly, battle gives lots of opportunities for "heroic" action and adventures, the kinds of things that some Shakespeareans say make for good plays. Erasmus, though, once again works against common sense understandings and argues the opposite:

> Soldiering, too, is a very energetic kind of idleness, and much the most dangerous, since it causes the total destruction of everything worthwhile and opens up a cesspit of everything that is evil. And so, if the prince will banish from his realm all such seed-beds of crime, there will be much less for his laws to punish.

It's a swift damnation built around the contradiction of "a very energetic kind of idleness." The soldier will seem to do lots – the kinds of activities celebrated in a play or film, perhaps – but those actions nevertheless amount to idleness. They create nothing and eventually lead to worse crimes. In Erasmus' treatment, war begets laziness. Peace inspires action. That is a central rethinking of peace, and it in turn opens up a realm of dramatic possibilities.

We're not saying that Shakespeare directly quotes lines from Erasmus' pacifist essays. It is true that Erasmus' work on peace was as popular as Machiavelli's on war during the period just before and during Shakespeare's lifetime. And we know that Erasmus' works were widely read in grammar schools. Further, scholars have argued for strong resonances of Erasmus' ideas and language in Shakespeare's plays. What we are saying is that peace movements have a long history, and Shakespeare's historical contemporaries thought about the very issues that haunt us today. They considered the costs and benefits of war, the associations of peace with effeminate laziness, and whether war follows from man's natural condition. Erasmus takes on a particularly adamant tone in his pacifism. In *The Education of a Christian Prince*, his summary is powerful: "The princes must set out to establish a perpetual peace among themselves and make common plans for it."[52] That ideal remains. And that political goal is intertwined with a dramatic point. If the plot cannot just end in peace, but actually explore peace, then Shakespeare will still have something to say in an era when many accept the logic of perpetual war.

We saw Obama struggle with the desire for peace while he admitted the unrelenting push for war. In so many ways, he is stuck in the same plot, the same narrative of World War II in which violence served the public good. Never mind that Obama cannot reconcile World War II with the standards of a just war. That is the cognitive trap of contemporary political thinking. Peacebuilding will require something else, a new narrative that Erasmus could endorse and that even Coriolanus might understand. Peace can indeed be imagined as an active condition, not just a stop but a beginning that is interesting and dramatic on its own.

Erasmus' two-word opening sentence helps. Peace speaks, and when Shakespeare is the one doing the writing, Peace will have plenty to say.

NOTES

1. She is quoted in Aric Jenkins, "Pro-Trump Protestors Interrupt 'Shakespeare in the Park' Performance of 'Julius Caesar'," *Time.com*, June 17, 2017, accessed August 2017.
2. Quoted in Rhys Blakely, "US drops 'mother of all bombs' on ISIS network in Afghanistan," *The Times* (London), April 14, 2017.
3. Ibid.
4. Quoted in Peter Baker and Choe Sang-Hun, "Trump Threatens 'Fire and Fury' Against North Korea if it Endangers U.S.," *The New York Times*, August 8, 2017, www.nytimes.com, accessed March 2018.
5. "Remarks by the President at the Acceptance of the Nobel Peace Prize," www.whitehouse.gov. All subsequent citations refer to this version of the speech.
6. Tony Zinni and Tony Koltz, *The Battle for Peace: A Frontline Vision of America's Power and Purpose* (New York: Palgrave Macmillan, 2006), 89.
7. "Remarks by the President on Ending the War in Iraq," October 21, 2011, www.whitehouse.gov.
8. Andrew J. Bacevich, *The Limits of Power: The End of American Exceptionalism* (New York: Metropolitan Books, 2008), 4.
9. Sarah Beckwith, *Shakespeare and the Grammar of Forgiveness* (Ithaca: Cornell University Press, 2011), 5.
10. Ibid., 6.
11. Ian Harris, Larry J. Fisk, and Carol Rank, "A Portrait of University Peace Studies in North America and Western Europe at the End of the Millennium," *International Journal of Peace Studies* 3.1 (1998).
12. Graham Holderness, *Shakespeare Recycled: The Making of Historical Drama* (New York: Harvester Wheatsheaf, 1992), 89–90.
13. Curtis C. Breight, *Surveillance, Militarism and Drama in the Elizabethan Era* (Basingstoke: Macmillan, 1996), 2, 38.
14. Edmund G. C. King, "'A Priceless Book to Have Out Here': Soldiers Reading Shakespeare in the First World War," *Shakespeare* 10.3 (2014): 230–44, 231.
15. Laurence Lerner, "Peace Studies: A Proposal," *New Literary History* 26.3 (1995): 641–65, 643.
16. Ibid., 647.
17. Paola Pugliatti, *Shakespeare and the Just War Tradition* (Burlington: Ashgate, 2010), 110.

18 Johan Galtung, "An Editorial," *Journal of Peace Research* 1.1 (1964): 2.
19 Johan Galtung, *Peace by Peaceful Means: Peace and Conflict, Development and Civilization* (London, Thousand Oaks, and New Delhi: SAGE Publications, 1996), 266.
20 Ibid., 9–10.
21 Ibid., 11.
22 Hugh Grady and Terence Hawkes, "Presenting presentism," in *Presentist Shakespeares*, ed. Hugh Grady and Terence Hawkes (New York: Routledge, 2007), 5.
23 Ibid., 5.
24 Madhavi Menon, *Unhistorical Shakespeare: Queer Theory in Shakespearean Literature and Film* (New York: Palgrave Macmillan, 2008), 2.
25 Ibid., 33.
26 Quoted in Bridget Elscome, *Emotional Excess on the Shakespearean Stage: Passion's Slaves* (London and New York: Bloomsbury, 2014), 34.
27 On the homoeroticism that runs throughout the film, see John Garrison, "Queer Desire and Self-Erasure in Coriolanus [2011]," *Literature Film Quarterly* 42.2 (2014): 427–37.
28 Quoted in Paola Pugliatti, *Shakespeare and the Just War Tradition* (Burlington: Ashgate, 2010), 103.
29 Ibid.
30 Andrew Hiscock, "'More Warlike Than Politique': Shakespeare and the Theatre of War – A Critical Survey," *Shakespeare* 7.2 (2011): 221–47, 240.
31 Quoted in Hiscock, 240.
32 Andrew J. Bacevich, *The New American Militarism: How Americans are Seduced by War* (New York: Oxford University Press, 2005), 2.
33 Niccolò Machiavelli, *The Prince*, 2nd Edn., trans. Robert M. Adams (New York: W. W. Norton & Co., 1992), 40.
34 Ibid., 40.
35 Ibid., 42.
36 See Robert P. Adams, *The Better Part of Valor: More, Erasmus, Colet, and Vives, on Humanism, War, and Peace, 1496–1535* (Seattle: University of Washington Press, 1962).
37 Desiderius Erasmus, "Dulce bellum inexpertis," in *Collected Works of Erasmus: Adages III.iv 1 to IV ii 100*, vol. 35, ed. John N. Grant, trans. Denis

L. Drysdall (Toronto: University of Toronto Press, 2001), 399–440, 400–1.
38 See Peter van de Dungen, "Erasmus: The 16th Century's Pioneer of Peace Education and a Culture of Peace," *Journal of East Asia and International Law* 2.2 (2009), 409–31, 429.
39 Erasmus, "Dulce bellum inexpertis," 401.
40 Ibid., 402.
41 Ibid., 407.
42 Desiderius Erasmus, "A complaint of peace spurned and rejected by the whole world," in *Collected Works of Erasmus: Literary and Educational Writings*, vol. 27, ed. A. H. T. Levi, trans. Betty Radice (Toronto: University of Toronto Press, 1986), 289.
43 Ibid., 310.
44 Richard Ned Lebow, *Why Nations Fight* (Cambridge: Cambridge University Press, 2010).
45 Ibid., 310.
46 Ibid., 310.
47 Desiderius Erasmus, *The Education of a Christian Prince*, ed. Lisa Jardine, trans. Neil M. Cheshire and Michael J. Heath (Cambridge: Cambridge University Press, 2010), 65.
48 Ibid., 103.
49 Ibid., 62.
50 Ibid., 98.
51 Ibid., 99.
52 Ibid., 97.

What's so funny 'bout peace, love, and understanding?

One

The music video for Elvis Costello and the Attractions' "(What's So Funny 'Bout) Peace, Love, and Understanding" opens with the four band members poised on the shore, their backs to the camera (Figure 1.1). It looks like they're pissing in the ocean. As the *Urban Dictionary* reminds us, "pissing in the ocean" indicates "a futile attempt; an act which will have very little or no consequence."[1] We have to ask ourselves, is this song of love and understanding going to be all about the futility of the peace movement? Not quite.

When the band members turn around, there's no zipping or buttoning of trousers. They've kept their hands in their pockets the entire time, fooling both camera and audience. This foursome did not come here to "piss in the ocean." It's a joke, but it's also a joke that asks us to be serious.

This cover of Nick Lowe's 1974 original appears on Elvis Costello and the Attractions' 1979 album *Armed Forces*, a title that invites us to think of musicians as a fighting unit. And the music video for "(What So Funny 'Bout) Peace, Love, and Understanding" itself constitutes an act of resistance. The crew filmed illegally after hours in Vancouver's Stanley Park – an act of civil disobedience that allowed the band to perform in front of Native totem poles, emblems of legacies of militaristic conflict and racist extermination that the song seeks to counteract.

Figure 1.1 Elvis Costello and the Attractions, a music video that gives us grainy footage of four guys who give a piss about peace ("(What's So Funny 'Bout) Peace, Love, and Understanding," Dir. Statler, Columbia Records, 1979)

In Nick Lowe's original, the sentiment reads as both hopeful and dismissive. After all, Lowe wrote it in 1974, at a time when the summer of love had run its course. His speaker is no wide-eyed counterculture youth, but an aging hippie looking out at a failing movement and wondering why his hopes are met with sarcastic sneers. When Costello got to the song a few years later, he turned the folk tune into an anthemic rocker for the 80s. That disparity, though, still speaks to the problematic opening of the video. Is Costello serious? Satirical? Can he be both? The resonances of the video posit just that potential. Although Costello and the Attractions may announce themselves with a joke, that joke need not undermine the sentiment that follows. Humor, in fact, may just help the plea for "peace, love, and understanding."

Shakespeare, of course, knew this. His comedies feature plenty of cynics rolling their eyes at the conventions of love. The point, however, remains: Peace emerges not in spite of those jokes, but because of them.[2]

This chapter focuses on two examples that even take care to suggest that nothing much happens in terms of plot. Characters waste time, play meaningless games, and take pleasure in idleness. In their titles, both *Much Ado About Nothing* and *As You Like It* make a point of being inconsequential, as if they say, "Go ahead and do whatever you want. It doesn't matter." That is precisely what makes them explorations of peace. The plays suggest an alternative to the formulation that the "schema of war and struggle, of the clash between forces, can really be identified as the basis of civil society."[3]

Another type of world is possible. That world isn't free from conflict. Instead, conflict becomes the basis of foolishness and triviality. And struggle, paradoxical though it seems, becomes the basis for peace.

NOTHING IS THE MATTER

Much Ado About Nothing makes clear its peacetime setting. Kenneth Branagh's 1993 film seizes onto the change from a time of war to a time of peace for all it's worth in the opening minutes. We watch the soldiers come thundering on horseback toward the camera, fresh from the battlefield and riding under their military banner (Figure 1.2). In a mirrored shot, the women of the town race toward home and excitedly prepare for their introductions. What follows is a rollicking and rambunctious sequence that sets the tone for the comedy to follow – a group bath with plenty of sexual implication

Figure 1.2 After the "action" but before the play (*Much Ado About Nothing*, Dir. Branagh, BBC Films, 1993)

(without actual sex). One soldier takes a slow-motion plunge into the tub; others strip off their uniforms and playfully splash one another; the women run water through their own hair and put on fresh dresses. The time for battle is over. Hit the showers and wash it all away.

At least that's how it starts.

Shakespeareans have often described Much Ado About Nothing as a secret "problem play" that feels more like a tragi-comedy than a fun romp. Even though it ends with marriages and smiling faces, the play gives us fake deaths and near murder along the way; the women remain unsettlingly powerless throughout. Despite any truce between nations, the bickering lovers Beatrice and Benedick continue to wage a "merry war" (1.1.50). Leonato says, "They never meet but there's a skirmish of wit between them" (1.1.50–51), a description that transfers the languages of war to this relationship. They may not actually inflict violence on each other, but they threaten, demean, and ridicule with aggression.

These undertones of violence lead many to think of *Much Ado About Nothing* as a troubling play, not nearly as funny as it's often performed. Benedick and Beatrice will be coerced into a marriage; Hero's father lashes out violently against his daughter without listening to her; and Claudio nearly murders multiple characters. War, we might assume, never goes away. While these characters may laugh and play the comedy, they never escape human cruelty, barely repressed misogyny, and threats of bloodshed.[4] This reading makes *Much Ado About Nothing* a cynical play, indeed. But that need not be the case. What Shakespeare reveals is a profound insight into "peace, love, and understanding," wrapped up in a bewildering paradox. The key line is spoken by Benedick, to his simultaneous lover and sworn enemy Beatrice: "Thou and I are too wise to woo peaceably" (5.2.61). Benedick ends up more right than even he knows; he understands that peace (and love) demand endless conflict.

The play's first lines underscore how the soldiers feel about the change to peacetime. Leonato, governor of Messina, receives the message that the war is over and that Don Pedro is coming with his soldiers in tow. Leonato asks, "How many gentlemen have you lost in this action?" (1.1.5). The war is literally the "action," which does mean military engagement in Shakespeare's day. "Action" also suggests something about the play that will follow. If the "action" is the violent stuff of masculine heroics, the remaining scenes will be "much ado about nothing." In *Hamlet*, the young prince often talks about "action" as what actors do when they perform. He first mentions the "actions that a man might play" (1.2.84), and he later tells the players staging *The Mousetrap* that when they put on their play, they should "suit the action to the word, the word to the action" (3.2.16–17). For Shakespeare, "action" means the kind of things audiences would expect upon entering the theater. *Much Ado About Nothing* subverts those expectations right away. The "action" is already over. Shakespeare's title announces the *Seinfeld* episode of the 16th century, daring us to care about a plot based on "nothing."

The plot kicks off with Claudio, a young soldier who just made a name for himself in battle. He recognizes a young woman who had caught his eye sometime in the past. He couldn't pursue her then, of course, because he was off to fight. Claudio tells his commander about his initial infatuation with Hero:

> When you [Don Pedro] went onward on this ended action
> I looked upon her with a soldier's eye,
> That liked, but had a rougher task in hand
> Than to drive liking to the name of love.
>
> (1.1.243–246)

Claudio repeats the word "action" in reference to the battle. Previously, he could see things only in terms of the fighter, but the battle is just now "ended," meaning that Claudio too can start looking at things in a different way. He can now pay attention to the boring and inconsequential. He even goes on to phrase his upcoming wooing as emptiness or vacancy, as more "nothing" in place of the war. He says,

> But now I am returned, and that war-thoughts
> Have left their places vacant, in their rooms
> Come thronging soft and delicate desires,
> All prompting me how fair young Hero is,
> Saying I liked her ere I went to wars.
>
> (1.1.247–251)

Finally, after the "action" of battle and masculine violence, the "delicate desires" allow Claudio to move toward affection and remind him of the woman he had met before, but his description of this shift depends upon emptiness. Love can enter the picture only once "war-thoughts/Have left their places vacant." Since nothing is happening, he can finally remember love.

Claudio continues this line of thinking when it comes time to get the girl. Critics have noticed that Claudio, vacant thoughts and all, does little of anything in these first scenes.[5] He says he loves Hero, but he leaves the rest to his commander Don Pedro, who says,

> If thou dost love fair Hero, cherish it,
> And I will break with her, and with her father,
> And thou shalt have her. Was't not to this end
> That thou began'st to twist so fine a story?
> (1.1.254–256)

So it's all to be arranged by others, and Don Pedro assumes that the "end" has already arrived. Claudio has remarked on the "ended" action of battle. Now, the love story seemingly has also reached its end, and without much of a show. That makes this love story fairly dull, but Claudio at least expresses some self-awareness when he remarks, "But lest my liking might too sudden seem/I would have salved it with a longer treatise" (1.1.260–261). Should he draw out the narrative? Try to seem more cautious, more patient, more active, if not more interesting? Don Pedro rejects the idea and says, "What need the bridge much broader than the flood?" (1.1.262). Why take more time and put in more work than is necessary? Shakespeare, then, plays with expectations of genre in these opening scenes. Peace and love are treated as emptiness, so the drama simply moves ahead. The audience never even hears what Don Pedro says to woo Hero. No need to waste the time.

When he gets the good news that Hero has accepted him, Claudio still doesn't seem to do much of anything. Don Pedro announces the marriage, and Leonato confirms his daughter's engagement. Claudio stands there without a word, a soldier unprepared for the fashions of civilian life. "Speak, Count, 'tis your cue" (2.1.266), Beatrice prods him. Claudio answers by doubling down on vacancy: "Silence is the perfectest herald of joy. I were but little happy if I could say how much" (2.1.267–268). Claudio presents his silence as celebratory, to which Hero answers with her own tight lips.

Hovering around the edges of the drama, another silent figure points toward the unsettling implications. Don John is the drama's villain, the brother who schemes to undo the marriage for no seeming good reason. He arrives with Don Pedro and is greeted alongside the rest of the soldiers. He responds with as good as silence: "I am not of many words, but I thank you" (1.1.127). Beatrice connects that reticence to the themes of the play as a whole. Don John is, she says, "too like an image and says nothing" (2.1.7–8). Another valence to the title *Much Ado About Nothing*. If it suggests initially "much ado about peacetime," here it shifts to suggest "much ado about the sadistic plans of this villain." Claudio is caught in between those meanings. He can't do anything on his own, and he is just as silent as Don John. The insinuation? He has more in common with Don John than he might want to admit. His silence is not just the "herald of joy" but a blank space in which paranoia and aggression can manifest.

This gap gives way to the even more striking bit of "nothing" in *Much Ado About Nothing* – Hero's suspected infidelity the night before her wedding to Claudio. Don John orchestrates the trap when he arranges for the waiting-woman Margaret to sleep with a minor henchman. Claudio will see this tryst from afar and think that it's Hero betraying him. This affair gives us yet another puzzling gap in the play since Shakespeare doesn't actually show us the scene. Don John insinuates that Hero is unfaithful and tells the others to meet him after midnight, when they can see someone enter her bedroom. We never get that moment. So we don't know exactly what drives Claudio to his cruel shaming of Hero at the wedding ceremony. Nothing, then, transforms from the moment of peaceful accord to the moment of paranoid projection. The gap – or the silence – is rendered a threat. Peace in turn fails.

When Claudio finally speaks, he attacks with violence. This is the only action he knows. The wedding begins with expected ceremonial lines from the Friar, but Claudio's responses turn "nothing" around to its cruel purpose. The Friar asks if anyone knows of "any inward impediment" (4.1.11) to the marriage. Leonato answers for Claudio: "I dare make his answer – none" (4.1.16). Claudio grows resentful and sarcastic when he asks his future father-in-law, "And what have I to give you back whose worth/May counterpoise this rich and precious gift?" (4.1.25–26). Don Pedro, knowing of Claudio's anger, steps in with some supporting viciousness: "Nothing, unless you render her again" (4.1.27). He means that Hero is worth nothing, and so there is no other gift worth the same. Critics have pointed out that "nothing" in Shakespeare's day could refer to women because they have "no thing." Certainly, Claudio's attack reveals his own deep sexism; he readily dismisses Hero as a "rotten orange" (4.1.30) without even giving her a chance. But "nothing" also follows from Claudio's own silence and vacant brain. He rejects Hero as "nothing" in the same way that he has already dismissed peacetime or love as nothing of importance. He curses his fiancée with "Hero itself can blot out Hero's virtue" (4.1.81). That is, Hero's virtue is erased by the actions of the unfaithful Hero. This woman is the new blank space, and as such, she is entirely dismissed from Claudio's world.

The wordplay on "nothing" continues as the play moves toward an ending that often feels less than comic. Trying to make Claudio feel regret, Hero's family spreads the rumor that she died from his accusations. It does no good for Claudio; she remains worthless, even in the grave. Don Pedro tells Hero's father and her uncle, "My heart is sorry for your daughter's death,/But on my honour she was charged with nothing/But what was true and very full of proof" (5.1.105–107). The "nothing" in his line cuts in two ways. On the surface, he does believe that nothing Claudio said is wrong. She is guilty. But the audience gets the underlying ironic meaning – Hero was charged with "nothing" true. Even though she committed no crimes, the "nothing" proves devastating. In the same scene, Leonato fumes at Claudio, almost to the point of outright violence:

Leonato: Marry, thou dost wrong me, thou dissembler, thou.
Nay, never lay thy hand upon thy sword,
I fear thee not.
Claudio: Marry, beshrew my hand
If it should give your age such cause of fear.
In faith, my hand meant nothing to my sword.

(5.1.52–56)

Shakespeare gives ambiguous stage directions in these lines. Leonato obviously finds some threat in Claudio, as if the young soldier began to draw his sword, ready to kill. Claudio maintains his innocence (ironic given what he did to Hero). He insists that he meant "nothing" in moving his hand to his weapon. This marks the near tragedy of Claudio's peaceful thinking. He doesn't intend violent warnings, but the "nothing" is treated as violent nonetheless. In not doing something, Claudio breaks the peace.

So here we are: *Much Ado About Nothing* translates to much ado about the implicit threats and dangers of silence, of vacant thought, of inactivity. Because Claudio assumes he's at peace, he enters war. The soldier's idleness is made belligerent. Claudio is at war or nothing else, so of course he always ends up fighting.

THERE'S SOMETHING ABOUT NOTHING

Beatrice and Benedick, the two lovers trapped in their "merry war," show us another way. Their plotline is familiar enough to fans of romantic comedy: Once these bickering foes are tricked into thinking the other is in love, they can overcome their superficial differences and finally come together. At the outset, however, their relationship feels impossible. That language of violent warfare dominates their exchanges, and at a more profound level, Benedick has no interest in the romantic trappings of peace. He mocks Claudio for exactly that behavior: "I have known when he would have walked ten mile afoot to see a good armour, and now will lie ten night awake carving the fashion of a new doublet" (2.3.14–16). Claudio has indeed given up his manly habits for the stuff of lovers. Benedick will have none of it, at least at first.

These early acts use the language of absence to mirror the couple's seeming lack of affection. In the same scene of Hero's engagement, Beatrice rejects all potential husbands. When Don Pedro makes a joking proposal to her, Beatrice makes a couple of jokes herself before answering, "I was born to speak all mirth and no matter" (2.1.288–289). She means that she never says anything of importance, just quips. We have another absence here, a "nothing" to go with Beatrice. In the scene where Beatrice learns of Benedick's supposed "love" for her, Hero gives almost the same account: "her wit/Values itself so highly that to her/All matter else seems weak" (3.1.52–54). She agrees with Beatrice; jokes are more important than anything that "matters."

What does this have to do with the love relationship? When Don Pedro describes the plot to bring Benedick and Beatrice together, he too uses the word "matter." He says, "The sport will be when they hold one an opinion of another's dotage, and no such matter" (2.3.191–193). The plot becomes fun, he means, when Benedick and Beatrice each think the other is in love. There will be no "such matter" to their love; it is based on nothing. What we see, then, is that the love between Benedick and Beatrice comes from nothing that you would typically associate with romance. Ironically, that "nothing" will make it stronger. Compare Hero and Claudio. When Don John first demeans Hero, Don Pedro asks, "What's the matter?" (3.2.72). Only about ten lines later, he exclaims again, "Why, what's the matter?" (3.2.83). It's her "infidelity" that matters, an unfaithfulness that Claudio and Don Pedro both eagerly believe. When something does finally "matter" in love, it works toward violence and destruction.

Benedick and Beatrice do better. Because they never "matter" in the way Claudio wants to matter, they can actually form something.

After Claudio denounces Hero, Beatrice has her heart-to-heart with Benedick. Notice the language they use to describe their utterly surprising romance. Benedick confesses, "I do love nothing in the world so well as you. Is not that strange?"

(4.1.266–267). Of course "nothing" has to show up again. The play always inverts what we expect of absence or vacancy. Just as the lack of action leads to violence, so it is that the lack of what "matters" leads to real affection, real attraction, real love. Beatrice answers Benedick with the same dizzying wordplay:

> As strange as the thing I know not. It were as possible for me to say I loved nothing so well as you, but believe me not, and yet I lie not. I confess nothing nor I deny nothing.
> (4.1.268–270)

Beatrice too loves "nothing" so well as Benedick, yet she also knows how implausible it all sounds. When she says his love is "as strange as the thing I know not," she plays with the idea of "stranger," but she's also playing with the idea of "thing." Their love is also a "thing I know not," a "no-thing" that nevertheless proves true. Beatrice will "confess nothing" nor "deny nothing," but the love remains. There is no matter here, and they love "nothing." In the play's logic, that works.

So that's why Benedick's line of peacefulness becomes so important. "Thou and I are too wise to woo peaceably" (5.2.61), he says. What makes the line so profound is that he grasps the subversion at which the play is always working. Their love isn't peaceful; that's what makes it actual love, actual peace. They admit wit and conflict; they admit that peace depends upon resolution of conflict rather than the absence of conflict. Claudio fundamentally cannot get this idea. Claudio's failures come from his misunderstandings of peacetime as a period of inactivity, absence, or nothing. The one who commits to the vacancy of peacetime never achieves it. Those who refuse to accept the end of action come to love.

This is peacetime for Shakespeare. Not the end of action, but the indulgence of conflict and wit. To woo peaceably, as Claudio and Hero try to do, only admits the paranoia and violent silence of Don John.

ANOTHER TAKE ON NOTHING: *AS YOU LIKE IT* AND THE BIG "IF"

In the most famous lines of *As You Like It*, the melancholy Jaques gives his description of life. "All the world's a stage," he says, before giving the seven scenes that inevitably end in old age. By then, everyone must face "mere oblivion,/Sans teeth, sans eyes, sans taste, sans everything" (2.7.138, 164–165). The speech doesn't exactly go for laughs.

Jaques – depressing though he may seem in this romantic comedy – finds his counterpoint in the play's clown, Touchstone. At a perhaps less well-known moment, Touchstone gives his accounting of the day, and he echoes "All the world's a stage" in his emphasis on inevitability and death. Needless to say, Jaques loves it. He actually reports the moment to the other characters who have been banished to the Forest of Ardenne. First, Touchstone took a sundial from his pocket:

> "It is ten of clock."
> "Thus we may see," quoth he, "how the world wags.
> 'Tis but an hour ago since it was nine,
> And after one hour more 'twill be eleven.
> And so from hour to hour we ripe and ripe,
> And then from hour to hour we rot and rot;
> And thereby hangs a tale."
>
> (2.7.22–28)

Time, in this account, simply goes on, and we could say that in some sense, Touchstone has described the entirety of life in the Forest of Ardenne. Separated from the court, this place does not provide much opportunity for "important" activities. As a space where repeated activities are continually enjoyed anew and idleness itself is a form of work, Shakespeare's play renders visible what Carolyn Dinshaw describes as "the possibility of a fuller, denser, more crowded now that all sorts of theorists tell us is extant but that often eludes our temporal grasp."[6] The people simply "ripe and ripe" and "rot and rot," listening to music and pissing into the ocean. Touchstone, though, is also a clever fool who never means exactly what he says. His description of the day includes plenty of sex puns. Hour by hour – or "whore by whore" – people get older, more experienced, and more depleted until the "tale" hangs limply. Jaques says that he "did laugh sans intermission/An hour by his dial" (2.7.32–33) after hearing Touchstone's diatribe. The sex jokes give some reasoning why, but we have to acknowledge that regardless, neither Jaques nor Touchstone are doing much but laughing for at least an hour. They embody the mood of the play – idle, sexual, unimportant, and cynical. Once again, nothing seems to be happening.

By the time the play reaches its ending, however, Touchstone reveals *As You Like It* as a play dedicated to simultaneous frivolity and serious meditations on peace. In the middle of explaining the proper etiquette of quarreling to Jaques, the clown gives an example:

> I knew when seven justices could not take up a quarrel, but when the parties were met themselves, one of them thought but of an "if," as "If you said so, then I said so," and they

shook hands and swore brothers. Your "if" is the only peace maker; much virtue in "if."

(5.4.88–92)

The anecdote of these judges, like much of Touchstone's wordplay, revels in the ludicrous. The "seven justices" cannot settle their fights by any direct means, which suggests their stubborn aggression. However, as soon as one proposes a hypothetical compromise, the quarrel dissolves. The beauty of the "if" comes from the way it allows the combatants to save face. All seven can agree to the peace, and because the terms only hypothesize, nobody has to give in. The solution functions in the same way as the continually postponed utopia of Lennon's "Imagine." The song does not demand that society must be religionless and warless immediately. Rather, it asks us to accept the possibility of such harmonious living. Lennon might elsewhere admit to being a violently "jealous guy," but even in that darker context he admits to such feelings being a problem of temporality.[7] "Jealous Guy" opens, "I was dreaming of the past," stressing that remaining steadfastly in the present now ripe with possibility of a better future is the pathway to peace.[8] Meditating on the relationship between performance and utopia, José Esteban Muñoz suggests that "the way to deal with the asymmetries and violent frenzies that mark the present is not to forget the future. The here and now is simply not enough."[9] The lesson – that sustainable peace requires negotiating between the momentary experience of tranquility and the promise that this break might predict a state of permanence – permeates the rest of Shakespeare's play.

It's no coincidence that the justices "shook hands and swore brothers," meaning they swore their brotherhood to one another. The play's main plot revolves around two sets of warring brothers. Duke Frederick usurped power from Duke Senior, and Oliver threatens death to his younger brother Orlando. In fact, Oliver's cruelty operates through an inversion of Touchstone's verbal peacemaker. He tells the wrestler Charles to take care in his match with Orlando: "If thou dost him any slight disgrace, or if he do not mightily grace himself on thee, he will practice against thee by poison, entrap thee by some treacherous device" (1.1.125–280). "If" emerges as the vehicle for defamation and violence just as much as peace. Charles echoes the same: "If he come tomorrow I'll give him his payment. If ever he go alone again, I'll never wrestle prize more" (1.1.134–136). For both villains, the ostensible "peacemaker" serves as the avenue toward violence. In this courtly environment, the hypotheticals allow no escape to new imaginative possibilities. Instead, "if" is the war hawk that imagines future threats that must be dealt with in the moment. The problem for Oliver, after all, comes from the threat of inheritance. Their father "charged [Oliver] on his blessing to breed [Orlando] well" (1.1.3), but Oliver also knows that Orlando is "all sorts of enchantingly beloved," especially by Oliver's "own people" (1.1.142–144). They fight, that is, over inheritance and the future. Orlando complains that he is marred by an enforced "idleness" (1.1.29) because he is barred what was promised. He desires a narrative with a future, and narratives – at least in this world – lead to poisonings and murder plots.

In the first moments in Ardenne, we witness the potentials of new, anachronistic narratives. Orlando arrives to the countryside after fleeing a life-threatening situation in Charles, the Renaissance hit man. Orlando, along with his serving man Adam, runs to the forest for safety, only to find himself on the brink of starvation.

That violent set-up turns suddenly when he arrives at the encampment of Duke Senior. Orlando ambushes the group with sword drawn, demanding food, but the conflict doesn't go as expected. Rather than answering violence with violence, Duke Senior tells Orlando that "your gentleness shall force/ more than your force move us to gentleness" (2.7.101–102). Here we see something like "passive resistance" practiced by Mohandas Gandhi or Martin Luther King, Jr. That is, beauty and kindness may be able to overpower physical threats. It also requires a new timeline, free of the threats of an inevitable, rotting future.

Because he has been groomed by the violence of the courtly world, Orlando engages the offer hesitantly. "I thought that all things had been savage here" (2.7.106), he explains. To try out this strange and peaceful way of living, he must first empathize, and to do so, he needs Touchstone's key word. Orlando says,

> But whate'er you are
> That in this desert inaccessible,
> Under the shade of melancholy boughs,
> Lose and neglect the creeping hours of time,
> If ever you have looked on better days,
> If ever been where bells have knolled to church,
> If ever sat at any good man's feast,
> If ever from your eyelids wiped a tear,
> And know what 'tis to pity, and to be pitied,
> Let gentleness my strong enforcement be,
> In the which hope I blush, and hide my sword.
> (2.7.108–118)

The whole thing rests on "if." Orlando accepts Duke Senior's invitation only when he can imagine that these vagabonds aren't really savages. In the series of hypotheticals, Duke Senior has learned pity and kindness. Orlando effectively says, "If you're the kind of people that know gentleness, then I can put my sword away." The language works, and Orlando becomes one with this strange commune. We should notice, too, that Orlando observes something else about the group: They don't care about time. Despite the insistence on time's inevitable passage in Jaques' "seven ages of man" speech, the forest court disrupts normative senses of time's relentless teleological thrust forward by neglecting "the creeping hours." The Duke and his men live like figures in the past and seem – if anything – to be "growing sideways," a phrase Kathryn Bond Stockton uses to emphasize that the insistence on "growing up" has limited our understanding of the transition from child to adult. Instead, she observes that "growth is a matter of extension, vigor, and volume, as well as verticality."[10] Indeed, both the peaceniks in the Forest of Ardenne and members of the peace movement in our more recent cultural memory seize upon childhood as a period that disrupts normative stories we tell ourselves about progress. Crosby, Stills, Nash, and Young's "Teach Your Children" (1970) frames the child as a means to interrupt, rather that perpetuate, our current way of life. "The Greatest Love of All" (originally recorded by George Benson in 1977 and later popularized by Whitney Houston) insists that "the children are our future" because their "laughter reminds us how we used to be." This understanding, where the future is a return to the past, should motivate us to "teach them well and let them lead the way." Curtis Mayfield's "We Have Got to Have Peace" (1971) repeats again and again the phrase "save the children" because "the little ones who just don't understand" will "help purify the land."[11] Achieving peace involves setting aside notions of the inevitability of forward movement and its march toward conflict over inheritance.

Even though Orlando accepts the invitation, he keeps his ability to cause harm within hand's reach: "I blush, and hide my sword." The perils of being exiled and nearly dying in the forest seem to have conditioned him to abide by the ancient Latin adage "*si vis pacem, para bellum*" ("if you want peace, prepare for war"). He'll behave as a gentleman and show his softer side, but he won't give up the blade just yet. This is the attitude of the *Pax Romana* or *Pax Brittanica* with which Shakespeare's audience would be familiar, a version of peace that substitutes security for true tranquility. And, as discussed throughout this book, it's a strand of thought that places the focus of "if" on the inevitability of war. The thinking is alive and well today.

We, like Orlando in this moment of the play, have become deeply wary of any promise of achieving peace in our time. Prime Minister Chamberlain famously used the phrase "peace for our time" in September of 1938 when he spoke in front of 10 Downing Street about the Munich Agreement and the Anglo-German Declaration. His speech ended with

> My good friends, for the second time in our history, a British Prime Minister has returned from Germany bringing peace with honour. I believe it is *peace for our time*. We thank you from the bottom of our hearts. Go home and get a nice quiet sleep.
>
> (our emphasis)

The reminder that this is "the second time" undermines any confidence that this peace can last. After all, this was the war that changed the name of the "Great War" or "the war to end all wars" to "World War I." Chamberlain's injunction to get a good night's sleep postulates the cyclicality of war and positions future conflict as something for which we must prepare. Yet the phrase "peace for our time" has staying power.[12] President Obama seized upon the phrase in his 2013 inaugural address, saying,

> we must be a source of hope to the poor, the sick, the marginalized, the victims of prejudice – not out of mere charity, but because *peace in our time* requires the constant advance of those principles that our common creed describes: tolerance and opportunity; human dignity and justice.
>
> (our emphasis)[13]

For Obama, the goal of sustainable peace can be achieved only on the domestic front. Conflict on foreign shores, we know, is positioned as inevitable.

As You Like It takes a much less cynical stance toward attaining peace in its audience's time, so long as Orlando can learn how to "neglect the creeping hours of time" (2.7.111). Indeed, the play's depiction of peace in the present looks backward *and forward* in time. In doing so, its Forest of Ardenne becomes ripe with potentiality and the virtue of "if." The ties between present and past become visible when Charles tells Oliver about the state of Duke Senior's court:

> They say he is already in the forest of Ardenne, and a many merry men with him; and there they live like the old Robin Hood of England. They say many young gentlemen flock to him every day, and fleet the time carelessly, as they did in the golden world.
>
> (1.1.99–103)

They've reclaimed the state of the Golden Age, a time of continual peace. The ancient Greek poet Hesiod's *Works and Days* (c. 700 BCE) describes the period as one when humans "lived like gods [and] dwelt in ease and peace."[14] Charles' description even suggests that peace was perpetuated through the Middle Ages by invoking Robin Hood. But the theatrical presentation is also about the audience's present, as Shakespeare names the forest after the woods near Stratford-Upon-Avon. He proposes that such a peaceful way of living in common may be nearby. Reflecting on the outlook for those fleeing a war-torn Syria, Slavoj Zizek suggests that such "refugees are possessed by a dream" and finds something deeply futile in their "enigmatic utopianism."[15] However, Shakespeare suggests that if audience members can "fleet the time carelessly," then peace "in our time" might just become peace for all time.

We can see that possibility in the miraculous conversions at the play's ending. After the viciousness of the villains in the play's opening, we learn that they have had sudden changes of heart, just like Touchstone's justices. The late-appearing and somewhat confusingly named Jaques de Bois gives this account of Duke Frederick's peaceful transformation:

> Duke Frederick, hearing how that every day
> Men of great worth resorted to this forest,
> Addressed a mighty power, which were on foot,
> In his own conduct, purposely to take
> His brother here, and put him to the sword.
> And to the skirts of this wild wood he came
> Where, meeting with an old religious man,
> After some question with him was converted
> Both from his enterprise and from the world,
> His crown bequeathing to his banish'd brother,

> And all their lands restored to them again
> That were with him exiled.
>
> (5.4.143–154)

It's not the most exciting of endings. Just when we might think a battle will erupt between brothers, an unknown hermit emerges to save the day. Jaques de Bois insists, "This to be true/I do engage my life" (5.4.154–155). It may be unbelievable, but "if" one can imagine it, peace is made possible.

The parity and equilibrium are underscored by productions, such as Kenneth Branagh's 2007 film version, that cast the same actor in the role of both Dukes.[16] In this version, Duke Frederick replaces a Zen Buddhist monk who appears early on to direct folks to the forest court.

We obtain an even stronger sense of this peaceful equilibrium when Duke Senior welcomes this second Jaques:

> Welcome, young man.
> Thou offer'st fairly to thy brothers' wedding:
> To one his lands withheld, and to the other
> A land itself at large, a potent dukedom.
> First, in this forest, let us do those ends
> That here were well begun and well begot.
> And after, every of this happy number
> That have endured shrewd days and nights with us
> Shall share the good of our returnèd fortune
> According to the measure of their states.
> Meantime, forget this new-fallen dignity
> And fall into our rustic revelry.
> Play, music, and you, brides and bridegrooms all,
> With measure heap'd in joy to th'measures fall.
>
> (5.4.155–168)

Here, the joyful "measure" in the last line applies both to the even distribution of property that will make amends and also to the music that will ensue as they engage in "rustic revelry." These measures ensure that "this happy number" will carry with them "potent dukedom" and "returned fortune" from the forest to the court. Even though courtly business may wait back home, in this piece of dialogue, the brothers remain in the forest just a little while longer.

Of course, not everyone has a place in the world that will ensue after the end of the play. Jaques announces that "to see no pastime, I. What you would have/I'll stay to know at your abandoned cave" (5.4.184–185). While some performances might have the rightful duke offer a pause of lament after Jaques' announcement, it does not seem to bother him much. After his exit, Duke Senior announces, "Proceed, proceed. We will begin these rites/As we do trust they'll end, in true delights" (5.4.186–187). The "rites" are multivalent, and they all contribute to peace-making. They include the wedding nuptials, the religious convictions of Frederick and the hermitic Jaques, and the "rights" to property that will be shared among the sons of Sir Roland de Bois (and in turn put in service of the court).

Does one of these approaches to peace supersede the others? Not necessarily. Commenters on a YouTube video of a live performance of "(What's So Funny 'Bout) Peace, Love, and Understanding" by Costello and Lowe have strong feelings about what makes for a good peace song and how this particular song should be performed. One user describes it as "a brilliant anti-war song better (and less schmaltzy) than [John Lennon's] 'Imagine'" but asserts that "Elvis' original version with the Attractions is still the best. It has to be done ANGRY!"[17] Another user responded, "I agree with everything except the fact that it 'has' to be done angry. I think this version's resignation and disappointment works just as well."[18] Shakespeare shares with these commenters the belief that there is more than one way to compose a peace anthem. Jaques will go to his cave. Frederick will join a religious order. The court will bind itself through a series of economic and social pacts. Yet the play's sudden shifts in character motivation – and its deliberate frustrations of audience expectations for the plot – reveal that these resolutions are in themselves temporary. By breaking the finality of tone, genre, and implication, Shakespeare disrupts the relentless march of time toward conflict. He shows "peace, love, and understanding" to be seriously funny and permanently temporary.

So what about the playgoers once they return from their respite here before the stage? The play's epilogue takes us out of the theatrical world and into the social world of the audience. In doing so, it engages in what performance studies scholar Richard Schechner describes as a circulatory and reciprocal relationship between social action and theatrical performance. Schechner suggests that "social drama" (the ways in which actions in the social sphere draw upon elements of theatrical performance) is always in dialogue with "aesthetic drama" (the ways in which theater performance takes raw material from actions in the social sphere).[19] Rosalind seems to have read her Schechner when she delivers the epilogue:

> It is not the fashion to see the lady the epilogue; but it is no more unhandsome than to see the lord the prologue. If it be true that good wine needs no bush, 'tis true that a good play needs no epilogue. Yet to good wine they do use good bushes, and good plays prove the better by the help of good epilogues. What a case am I in then, that am neither a

good epilogue nor cannot insinuate with you in the behalf of
a good play! I am not furnished like a beggar, there-fore to
beg will not become me. My way is to conjure you;

[. . .]

And I charge you, O men, for the love you bear to women –
as I perceive by your simpering none of you hates them –
that between you and the women the play may please. If
I were a woman I would kiss as many of you as had beards
that pleased me, complexions that liked me, and breaths
that I defied not. And I am sure, as many as have good
beards, or good faces, or sweet breaths will for my kind
offer, when I make curtsy, bid me farewell.

(Epilogue, 1–19)

Rosalind reminds audience members that they have been part of the peace shared while they watched the drama past the edge of the proscenium. As Helga Duncan observes, the play's epilogue "alludes to the heterotopic function of the theater where fantasy, discourse, and actors' bodies interconnect and generate space."[20] And members of the audience now too have the opportunity to seize upon Touchstone's big "if." If this actor were a woman – which he's not in Shakespeare's day – then she would please her audience as much as they please her. That hypothetical collapses the dualism of gender and the dualism of good/bad plays. It also gives everyone the chance to find pleasure, "to like as much of this play as please you." Rosalind, in her cross-dressing throughout the play, has already disrupted norms of courtship and by implication the norms of patriarchal inheritance. Her epilogue allows those disruptions to persist, to admit that the audience is just as subject to temporary shifts in appreciation, gender, and action.

While the epilogue resonates with Schechner's notion of the circulation of behaviors between the theatrical and social worlds, it also seems to give voice to the focus on "if" in Constantin Stanislavski's system of acting. The early 20th-century method instructed actors to walk through a series of "what if" scenarios for their characters in order to find the "truth" of the character within themselves.[21] The audience, ultimately, is "conjured," made to find peace in Rosalind's "if." It's a clever, funny ending. And it suggests the real-world potential for peace in ignoring time, joking, and staying in the forest as a state of mind. By effectively pissing into the ocean, Rosalind makes a case for the importance of peace, love, and understanding.

NOTES

1 "Pissing in the Ocean," *Urban Dictionary*, Web, July 6, 2015.

2 Daniel Juan Gil has argued recently that the tragedies are critical for our understanding of Shakespeare's attitudes toward politics because they depict "the generative, productive potential of the experience of being utterly and inescapably exposed to state power" (10). Steven Marx, too, chooses to survey the tragedies when seeking to trace Shakespeare's attitudes toward peace. We look instead to the comedies to imagine states where, as John Lennon puts it, "there's no countries / [. . .] / Nothing to kill or die for." Daniel Juan Gil, *Shakespeare's Anti-Politics: Sovereign Power and the Life of the Flesh* (New York: Palgrave MacMillan, 2013), John Lennon, "Imagine," by John Lennon, Imagine, Apple Records (1971), and Steven Marx, "Shakespeare's Pacificism," *Renaissance Quarterly* 45.1 (Spring 1992): 49–95.

3 Michel Foucault, *"Society Must Be Defended": Lectures at the Collège de France 1975–76*, trans. David Macey (New York: Picador, 2003), 18.

4 So literary critic Susan Harlan argues, "By subsuming the soldiers into their society, Messina tacitly absorbs their military history and transforms it into a set of values that signify for masculine character in the context of comedy," in "'Returned from the Wars': Comedy and

Masculine Post-war Character in Shakespeare's Much Ado About Nothing," Upstart (2013). In other words, the men will take what they learn in the military and apply it to the marriage. There is no real difference between peace and war.

5 Mark Taylor, for example, says that Claudio plays the "triumphant suitor" without "doing much of anything," in "Presence and Absence in Much Ado About Nothing," *Centennial Review* 33.1 (1989): 1–12.

6 Carolyn Dinshaw, *How Soon Is Now? Medieval Texts, Amateur Readers, and the Queerness of Time* (Durham: Duke University Press, 2012), 4.

7 Jaques associates envy and militarism when he describes the age of "soldier" at which a man becomes "jealous in honor, sudden and quick in quarrel" (2.7.150).

8 John Lennon, "Jealous Guy," by John Lennon, Imagine, Apple Records (1971).

9 José Esteban Muñoz, *Cruising Utopia: The Then and There of Queer Futurity* (New York: NYU Press, 2009), 96.

10 Kathryn Bond Stockton, *The Queer Child, or Growing Sideways in the Twentieth Century* (Durham: Duke University Press, 2009), 11.

11 Each of these songs may draw upon the depiction of the Day of the Lord in Isaiah 11:6, where "the wolf shall dwell with the lamb, and the leopard shall lie down with the young goat, and the calf and the lion and the fattened calf together; and a little child shall lead them."

12 The phrase has appeal not just in recent politics but also in popular music. There are at least ten original songs with "Peace in Our Time" as the title, including a 1938 Christian hymn and a 1989 hard rock version from Russian band Gorky Park, as well as pop songs by Elvis Costello (1984) and Ray Davis (2007).

13 Barack Obama, "Inaugural Address by President Barack Obama," *United States Capitol*, January 21, 2013, whitehouse.gov, accessed 6 July 2015.

14 Hesiod, *Works and Days in The Homeric Hymns and Homerica with an English Translation*, trans. Hugh G. Evelyn-White (Cambridge, MA: Harvard University Press, 1914), lines 115 and 120.

15 Zizek describes Syrian refugees as arriving in southern Italy only to long to be in Scandinavia as evidence for their fantasy-driven craving for a peace that is always out of reach because "the hard truth to be faced by the refugees is that 'there is no Norway,' even in Norway." Slavoj Zizek, "The Non Existence of Norway," *London Review of*

Books, September 9, 2015, www.lrb.co.uk/2015/09/09/slavoj-zizek/the-non-existence-of-norway

16 *As You Like It*, dir. Kenneth Branagh, perf. Bryce Dallas Howard, Kevin Kline, Romola Garai, Adrian Lester (Shakespeare Film Company, 2007).

17 Geoffrey Waring, "Re: Elvis Costello & Nick Lowe Live," *YouTube*, accessed July 6, 2015.

18 Bob Fenster, "Re: Elvis Costello & Nick Lowe Live," *YouTube*, accessed July 6, 2015.

19 Schechner takes up the notion of "social drama" from Victor Turner and adds "aesthetic drama" as a component always in dialogue with the former. Both Schechner and Turner view the relationship between performance in the theater and performance in the social sphere as reciprocal, though Schechner interprets the two as being closer to equilibrium than does Turner. For the first formulation of this relationship as a diagram, see Richard Schechner, "Selective inattention," in *Essays on Performance Theory 1970–1976* (New York: Drama Books, 1977), 144.

20 Helga L. Duncan, "'Here at the Fringe of the Forest': Staging Sacred Space in As You Like It," *Journal of Medieval and Early Modern Studies* 43.1 (Winter 2013): 138.

21 Stanislavski, an actor and director with the Moscow Art Theater, developed the system beginning in the 1910s. It integrated Theodule Ribot's concept of "affective memory" and was articulated by several people who worked with Stanislavksi as well as in his 1936 *An Actor Prepares*. For more detail see Constantin Stanislavski, *An Actor Prepares*, trans. Elizabeth Reynolds Hapgood (London and New York: Methuen, 1986) and Colin Counsell, *Signs of Performance: An Introduction to Twentieth-Century Theatre* (London and New York: Routledge, 1996), 1–23.

Make love, not war
Two

Spike Lee's 2015 film *Chi-Raq* was marketed with a simple tagline: "No peace, no piece." The movie updates the plot of Aristophanes' *Lysistrata*, first performed in Athens in the 5th century BCE. In the ancient comedy, the women of Greece refuse to sleep with their husbands and lovers until the men stop fighting in the Peloponnesian war. In Lee's film, a modern-day group of women (and a few men identified as being on the "down low") refuse sex with their male partners until gang violence ends on the south side of Chicago, a neighborhood (the film tells us during its opening sequence) that is plagued by so many gun deaths that it constitutes a war zone. In fact, the film takes its title from a real-world nickname; "Chicago" has become the latest "Iraq." Like the ancient play upon which it is based, *Chi-Raq* makes its points about peace through comedy (an approach that did draw criticism from some viewers). The women chant "no peace, no pussy" while dancing in the streets, wearing camouflage outfits or sporting elaborate chastity belts. These outfits alert us to the evocative intersection between sexuality and war, as do numerous puns that conflate sex and violence.

It is, of course, not a new idea to think about love and war as intertwined. If we say "love is a battlefield," more than a few readers surely will find themselves fondly recollecting Pat Benatar's 1984 Grammy Award–winning power ballad.

Indeed, the music video for that song presages *Chi-Raq* in its scenes of costumed dancers taking to the streets to express dissatisfaction with social norms. After the unison choreography in the street, the women embrace, underscoring how shared passion about social issues can strengthen interpersonal, affective bonds (Figure 2.1).

The notion that the marital and the martial share close kinship can be traced at least back to ancient Athens, where the women of the *Lysistrata* claim it is fair to withhold sex in times of war. Lysistrata herself addresses her allied women as "dear comrades" and urges them, "let us not give up the fight, hard though it is to endure."[1] Scenes of pacifist determination such as these speak to the notion of "positive peace." They dramatize Johan Galtung's definition of peace as "what we have when creative conflict transformation takes place nonviolently."[2]

Figure 2.1 Hugging it out ("Love Is a Battlefield," Dir. Giraldi, GASP! Productions, 1983)

Shakespeare does not shy away from the same evocative overlap between love and war that we have begun to trace here across film, drama, and popular song. Indeed, early modern literature offers a particularly rich archive for exploring this overlap. Work by Melissa Sanchez recently has traced a "commonplace early modern equation of political and erotic unions," and, in turn, she invites us to complicate the nature of both love and politics.[3] In Shakespeare's *Henry IV Part One* (1598), for example, Henry's rival Hotspur describes his sexual exploits as to "tilt with lips" (2.4.84), deploying the language of jousting to describe erotic encounters with female genitalia. In *Coriolanus*, Aufidius takes one look at the man who is his mortal enemy, and declares, "Thou noble thing, more dances my rapt heart/Than when I first my wedded mistress saw/Bestride my threshold" (4.5.115–117). Sanchez's work and these instances from the plays urge us to understand the complexities of early modern texts where love and war intersect. This mixing of sex and violence shows up not just in the histories and tragedies but in the comedies too. It's hard not to see the antics of *Taming of the Shrew* (1590–1594) as a tale of love as a battlefield. In a wonderful image from the Folger Shakespeare Library in Washington DC, an American soldier in Vietnam carries a copy of the play in his helmet.

It's tempting to speculate whether he found the comedy a welcome balm for the violence of war or more gas for the fire.[4] Modern audiences might find disquieting Petruchio's strategies of withholding food and sleep from Katherine in *The Taming of the Shrew* in order to win her submission as wife. The ambiguous resolution of the play can feel like the romantic comedy version of "Stockholm syndrome" in many ways.

Early modern audiences were not unaware that Petruchio's treatment of Katherine would disquiet some people. In 1611,

Shakespeare's contemporary and sometime collaborator John Fletcher composed a sequel to Taming of the Shrew entitled The Woman's Prize, or the Tamer Tamed.[5] The play describes how Petruchio's tumultuous marriage to Katherine ended in her death, and the story opens with him re-married.[6] In order to convince him to change his taming ways, the new bride and a group of other local women take a page from Lysistrata and refuse sex with their husbands until the men curb their violent tendencies.

The plot of Fletcher's play could sound so extreme as to be only the stuff of fiction, designed to make theater-goers laugh at "the war of the sexes."[7] But this plot that we see carried across Chi-Raq, Lysistrata, and The Tamer Tamed has real purchase on pacifist efforts in our contemporary culture. There have been several major "sex strikes" for peace in the 20th and 21st centuries, including ones in Colombia, the Philippines, the South Sudan, and Liberia.[8] This last example, led by Leymah Gbowee and the Women of Liberia Mass Action for Peace, gives Spike Lee's own Lysistrata the idea for her sex strike to end local gang violence when she finds a video online of Gbowee touting the success of the Liberian campaign. While the highly choreographed and costumed street performances in Chi-Raq adopt tropes of Hollywood musicals, they recollect the place that songs often have in protest movements. Take, for example, this 2006 rap song by sex strikers in Pereira, Colombia:

> *Como mujer, mucho valemos*
> *que no nos deslumbre, un hombre violento*
> *porque con ellos, mucho perdemos.*
> *Yo elijo cómo, dónde, cuándo me entrego.*
> *Todas unidas lo lograremos*

contra los violentos, las piernas cerremos.
Paro sexual,
paro sexual!

[As women, we have great worth
A violent man will not impress us
Because with them, we lose so much.
I will choose how, where, when I submit myself.
All together, we will win
Against the violent ones, we close our legs
Sex strike
Sex strike!][9]

The erotic refusals at the heart of these campaigns play a clear role in social change efforts. Gbowee and two other women were granted the Nobel Peace Prize in 2001 for what the selection committee lauded as their gains toward achieving "democracy and lasting peace in the world."[10] Lee's film nods to the cross-cultural appeals of the sex strike, as the Chicago women ignite a series of global protests, depicted as news footage of women chanting "no peace, no pussy" in various languages around the world.

The effectiveness of a sex-strike campaign, in part, is its status as spectacle. Gbowee relates that the sex strike "had little or no practical effect, but it was extremely valuable for getting us media attention."[11] It is a reminder of how theatrical performance and social activism are continually in dialogue with each other.[12] The relationship is captured nicely in a concept we have already introduced: the "Shechner Loop," which describes a circulatory and reciprocal relationship between social action and theatrical performance. Recall that performance studies scholar Richard Schechner suggests that "social drama" (the ways in which actions in the social sphere draw upon elements of theatrical performance) is always in dialogue with "aesthetic drama" (the ways in which theater performance draws raw material from actions in the social sphere). Spike Lee wonderfully dramatized the flow of the "Schechner Loop" after the premiere of *Chi-Raq*. Instead of hosting an after-party, Lee presented attendees with matching orange knit hats – symbols of the gun-control movement – and led them out of Manhattan's Ziegfeld Theater on a march down Broadway to Times Square to protest gun-violence. His film, inspired by previous literature and featuring a protagonist who inspires global protests that resemble the real-world sex strikes, becomes a flashpoint for how art and life imitate each other. The celebration-turned-march blurs the line between the worlds inside and outside of the film, while underscoring that art can turn desire for change into action.

What we find particularly interesting about a sex strike is that it places erotic desire in opposition to war, rather than relying on the familiar truisms and pop songs that ask us to see them as the same thing. *If you keep fighting, you will not have sex*, the strikers insist. In that, we can hear resonances of the well-known 1960s peace slogan "Make Love, Not War," which advocates sex as an alternative to fighting. You can be a lover rather than a fighter, and that can make you a hero. Accepting that logic involves accepting an increasingly complex understanding of love and of what "fighting" entails, especially being willing to include a concept of viable force at work in social protest rather than just in military or police action. Faced with a crowd of anti-war protesters sporting signs with the slogan when he was governor of California, Ronald Reagan once quipped, "Their signs say 'make love, not war.' But they don't look like they could do much of either."[13] His biographer, Dinesh D'Souza, suggests that Reagan saw the peace demonstrators as incapable of real action and too unkempt to be attractive. The line sounds like a dig at the concept of "waging peace" or "peace in action," seemingly paradoxical concepts at the heart of Peace Studies. You're not a real man or woman unless you can have sex *and* make war, like a movie action hero. However, as we have begun to show, sexual desire has a role not only in war-making but also in the peace-making and peace-sustaining process, both in the literary imaginary and in the sphere of social action.

To begin to understand how "Make Love, Not War" might actually work, one must accept that love has a place in the public, political sphere in which we debate (and make and fund) war. At first, it might be hard to do. Hannah Arendt thought that we couldn't even talk about love in connection to politics. Love, she claimed, "is not only apolitical but antipolitical, perhaps the most powerful of all antipolitical human forces."[14] Her dismissal assumes a certain kind of love, one that is basically private in nature. However, we can resist such a blanket dismissal of love's place in politics when we consider, for example, the distinction between public and private forms of love, which Michael Hardt depicts nicely:

> Our intimate notions of love and our social notions are generally held to be radically separate and even divergent. The love of the couple and the family, for example, the dominant conceptions of love in our current vocabulary, are most often considered to be a private affair, whereas love of country, probably the most widely recognized public form of love today, is most often seen as operating outside the sphere of intimacy.[15]

When activists use the slogan "Make Love, Not War," they challenge these commonplace assumptions and deliberately intermingle the public with the private. They are not simply saying, "love other countries, don't war against them." That's too close to the logic of why we *do* go to war with other countries – because love of the nation is so often bound up in violence toward others. Nationalistic love shares with romantic love the quality of being, as one recent scholar in the field of affect studies, Sara Ahmed, puts it, a "sticky emotion," one that "sticks the nation together; it allows cohesion through the naming of the nation or 'political community' as shared object of love."[16] Such love, of course, can be deployed to legitimize warfare. Love has the propensity to both separate us from others and to bring us together. But just as love confuses categories, for example, the distinction between the "I" and "you" in the loving couple, it also productively confuses distinctions between public and private.

Ahmed's notion of love as a "sticky emotion" resonates in the famous "Saint Crispin's Day Speech" from Shakespeare's *Henry V*. The king, on the verge of a battle with France where the English will be vastly outnumbered, celebrates the love of soldiers fighting side-by-side for their country:

> We few, we happy few, we band of brothers.
> For he today that sheds his blood with me
> Shall be my brother; be he ne'er so vile,
> This day shall gentle his condition.
> And gentlemen in England now abed
> Shall think themselves accursed they were not here,
> And hold their manhoods cheap whiles any speaks
> That fought with us upon Saint Crispin's day.
>
> (4.3.60–67)

Because these men will shed their blood for a common cause, they become brothers. Henry uses anaphora, repeating "we" in successive phrases to emphasize that the men's status will be elevated toward parity with the sovereign, the value of which is emphasized by the first line encompassing an extra syllable. The power of the speech – and the ways in which the phrase "band of brothers" subsequently has been taken up in modern depictions of war – reminds us that the terms of familial love, which we often associate with the private space of the home, can be translated to the public experience of being bonded with strangers. Jasbir Puar's notion of "homonationalism" resonates here, as the bonds of sameness between the men constitute an acceptable form of love that binds them to each other and ultimately serves England's investment in imperial expansion and, indeed, heterosexual reproduction.[17] In the speech, we find echoes of Reagan's comments about the peace activists when Henry turns his attention to those men who stayed in bed at home rather than fighting in the battle. By saying that they will "hold their manhoods cheap," a colloquialism that the *Oxford English Dictionary* tells us was coined in the 17th century to indicate "to hold of small account, to think little of," the king not only implies that these other men are not as masculine as the "band of brothers" but also discredits them as lovers. Henry assures his men that their ability to conquer on the battlefield will make them conquerors in the bedroom.

"Make Love, Not War" refuses Henry's logic and celebrates those who stay at home. If he wants to say that fighting at Agincourt gives the soldier his "manhood," the peace activist in contrast says that fighting gets in the way of a more robust form of sexuality for those who embrace peace and peace-making. Lauren Berlant, writing a response to Michael Hardt's essay that we have just quoted, suggests that "love is one of the few situations where we desire to have patience for what isn't working, an affective binding that allows us to iron things out, or to be elastic, or to try a new incoherence."[18] This is the promise of love: We're changed by it, and we're willing to change for it. More than that, we're willing to be uncomfortable and to admit weakness on our own part. Our desire for love can help us overlook infringements upon us. Contemporary couples know the standard line of advice: "Don't go to bed angry."[19] Henry makes the bed a place of anger. Only men can make love, and they're only men if they fight. Thankfully, Shakespeare didn't stop with Henry.

COMPLICATING LOVE'S RELATIONSHIP TO WAR IN *LOVE'S LABOUR'S LOST*

In other works, Shakespeare embraces the tantalizing calculus where love — with its attendant qualities of compromise, consent, and mutuality — might be powerful enough to defeat our warring impulses and make us the better for it. If we give "Make Love, Not War" a chance, it does have a visceral appeal. The slogan might as well ask, "wouldn't you rather be making love right now?" However much we might love our jobs, schoolwork, or even making war, it is likely that most of us would rather be in bed with someone whose intimate company we'd enjoy. Especially when we're first discovering love – whether as teenagers or in the early phases of any relationship – love pulls us away from other activities. As Romeo puts it,

> Love goes toward love as schoolboys from their books,
> But love from love, toward school with heavy looks.
> (2.1.201–202)

Love is such a wonderful and deliciously tempting distraction. Indeed, Shakespeare often follows this line of thinking:

Just when things seem utterly predictable and under one's own control, love comes along to take characters in a new direction. Like schoolboys plodding to the classroom, they can ditch their plans and find other ways to spend their days.

In fact, Romeo's lines very nicely summarize the plot of one of Shakespeare's earliest plays, *Love's Labour's Lost* (1598). In it, love defeats Ferdinand, the King of Navarre, and three of his noblemen. The group take vows of chastity, announcing at the play's start that they will not allow any women within a mile of their court in order to dedicate themselves to three years of study. The king tells his fellows:

> Therefore, brave conquerors – for so you are,
> That war against your own affections
> And the huge army of the world's desires –
> Our late edict shall strongly stand in force.
> Navarre shall be the wonder of the world.
> Our court shall be a little academe,
> Still and contemplative in living art.
>
> (1.1.8–14)

They sound like gods of war who have announced they can beat Love. They boast of being "conquerors" even before they have beaten the incredible odds and "huge army" of desires ready to stand against them. In the service of self-mastery, they commit to resisting the many things that they might desire as well as those things or people who might desire them.

It doesn't last long.

It is as if, despite their dedication to studies, the noblemen of Navarre have never heard that love conquers all. It is funny that the men in *Love's Labour's Lost* present their version of a sex strike as going to war with their affections. Whereas the women in *Chi-Raq* want to use the sex strike to achieve peace, the men think of their sex strike as another kind of war. They want to "Make War, Not Love," and it's a battle we know they can't win. And it seems all the more futile because we know that the sex they deny themselves is one of those, as Adam Phillips terms them, "unforbidden pleasures." Sex simply does not need the "language of control, of discipline and punishment."[20] Of course, sex has historically been subject to these mechanisms, but in the "free love" of the romantic comedy, such rules are often self-imposed and meant to be broken. In *Love's Labour's Lost*'s comic subplot, a fop named Adriano de Armado falls in love with a beautiful woman. He also describes this romance in martial terms:

> I will hereupon confess I am in love; and as it is base for a soldier to love, so am I in love with a base wench. If drawing my sword against the humour of affection would deliver me from the reprobate thought of it, I would take desire prisoner and ransom him to any French courtier for a new-devised curtsy.
>
> (1.2.53–58)

He's already re-writing the logics of the conquerors who are on their sex strike. He knows that to fight is futile, that he cannot use his sword to fend off love. As if questioning his own manhood, he asks his servant, "Comfort, me, boy. What great men have been in love?" (1.2.59–60). The servant responds with examples of Hercules and Samson. This seems like good company for a base soldier. These men are strong warriors. One is the son of Zeus, and the other is imbued with superhuman strength by the God of the Bible. Gods among men, they (and perhaps now Adriano too) are in the company of

Mars. For a brief moment, Adriano can be in love and make war.

While Adriano fights for his beloved, the four cloistered noblemen have their plans foiled by the arrival of four noblewomen from France. They woo. Gifts are given. Jokes are exchanged. There's a masquerade ball. It all seems to be going smoothly toward a typical comedic ending with four marriages until news arrives that the King of France has died. The four women, who include the princess of France, must go home to mourn. It certainly doesn't sound like the ending for which we were being set up. Some scholars believe that audiences were so dissatisfied with the ending that Shakespeare wrote a sequel. We do know that a play existed by Shakespeare with the title *Love's Labour's Won*, but it is now considered lost.

Kenneth Branagh's film version of *Love's Labour's Lost* (2000) gives us a stronger sense of an ending. It places the story in the 1940s and transforms Shakespeare's play into a musical filled with dance numbers to standards by Irving Berlin and Cole Porter. The film also adds the specter of the looming world war. Like that of the original play, the film's wooing is cut short with the news that the King of France has died, but the adaptation introduces subsequent news that France has fallen to the Nazis. The film then transmits details of what happens to the characters after parting. In black-and-white newsreel, we see each of the lovers take roles in the war and then watch them reunite on V-E Day.[21] The film ends with a freeze-frame of the couples reunited. At first, it crystallizes as a black-and-white photo. Then it transitions to color. It's a reminder that the moment it depicts – soldiers returning home from war, love's victory in uncertain times – is just as poignant in the present era of the viewer as it has been in the past. Interestingly, the film's final sequence is choreographed to George and Ira Gershwin's "You Can't Take That Away From Me" (1937). The choice of tune stresses once again that war can't conquer love. Some things — like the unforbidden pleasure of love and our belief that peacetime can be achieved again — can't be taken away from us. The song's title and its sentiment ultimately contradict the title of the play, letting us know that the labor toward love was not truly lost in this story. Such losses were only temporary.

The idea that the lovers will reunite after the separation that concludes *Love's Labour's Lost* is not unique to Branagh's adaptation, nor is the notion that this play about a sex strike is haunted by the ghost of war. In 2014, the Royal Shakespeare Company (RSC) staged the play and set it in 1914, distinctly within the early days of World War I. During the same production season, the RSC staged a play under the title *Love Labour's Won* and set it at the end of the war in 1918. This supposed sequel to *Love's Labour's Lost* was a fitting companion in conversations about peace. What the RSC titled *Love's Labour's Won* was the play we know as *Much Ado About Nothing*, a play that some scholars believe to be Shakespeare's intended sequel to *Love's Labour's Lost*. It is interesting that the RSC chose to commemorate World War I by staging a play about men who must leave their women and then staged a play about men returning home after victory. The second play's narrative isn't just about the impulse to return to love, though. As we've seen in the previous chapter, *Much Ado About Nothing* has a lot to tell us about sustainable peace in the middle of conflict.

THE GODDESS OF LOVE TAMES THE GOD OF WAR

One of Shakespeare's earliest works complicates the relationship between making love and making war. In the poem *Venus and Adonis*, Shakespeare plays on the well-known phrase *amor vincit omnia*, love conquers all, as he dramatizes the power of the goddess of love, Venus, over a young man who prefers hunting and killing wild animals to love-making. "*Amor vincet omnia*" is an old adage often attributed to the ancient poet Virgil's *Eclogues* (44–38 BCE), a group of pastoral poems that include the prediction that the new Golden Age was upon us. Virgil depicts that endless spring when peace reigned on Earth. Ancient and early modern writers described the Golden Age as an actual past that could, in turn, be recaptured. Virgil's famous phrase, combined with his promise that this period of lasting peace would come again, suggests that love might make us give up our warring ways.

During her attempts to seduce Adonis, the goddess of love relates a time when she seduced the god of war. Mars was so moved by his desire for Venus that "Over my altars hath he hung his lance,/His battered shield, his uncontrollèd crest" (103–104). He abandons his weapons and his ways of being that seem to be wearing on him. And he does so by abandoning his past (the past-tense "battered") and his recklessness (his state of being "uncontrolled"). Instead, he learned "to sport and dance,/To toy, to wanton, dally, smile, and jest" (105–106). It is not just that he becomes more carefree (though that's an important part of his new self). He also learns elements of *performance*. He demonstrates his love for Venus by sporting and dancing, and these activities replace battle. Venus describes how she convinced this gentler Mars to begin "making my arms his field, his tent my bed" (108). He no longer needs to take up arms because he has her arms to hold him. He no longer needs to pitch a tent on the battlefield. He can do that between the sheets.

Mars makes a series of changes for love, and these changes track to the kinds of distinctions we are drawing here between tragedy and comedy, between pernicious violence and playful spectacle. That is, he embraces new ways of being and doing that can be just as rewarding as martial conquest. Venus describes how "he that over-ruled I overswayed" (109). The transition from *ruling* to *swaying* involves a movement from a form of influence based in force to one based in persuasion. When she describes "leading him prisoner in a red-rose chain" (110), we hear the type of play and costume that are the stuff of comedic theater: turning expectations on their ear, clowning around in the pursuit of pleasure. Her final claim to victory is that she "foiled the god of fight" (114). It's a telling turn of phrase. We can think of "foil" as signaling his exchange of a deadly sword for the type used in the sport of fencing. But we can also think of love as war's "foil." That is, love is a kind of opposite that also has elements of what it opposes. Love ultimately overcomes the embodiment of war won by showing him just how romantic passion can deliver all of the rewards of military conflict but in more nuanced ways.

While that might be the end of Venus' story about Mars, it is not the end of Shakespeare's *Venus and Adonis*. In the poem, *love does not conquer all*, resulting in a scorned Venus issuing a prophecy, "[Love] shall be cause of war and dire events,/ And set dissension 'twixt the son and sire" (1159–1160). This startling claim suggests that *making love makes war*. And, while we might appreciate how her fierce stance resists a too-frequent tendency to essentialize women as inherently peaceful, such an ending may leave readers wondering if it isn't safer just to keep love out of the public and political sphere, lest it have destructive consequences. Yet, what love offers us is its unique tendency to bounce back and to make us open to second chances. Given how we've seen Mars change for love or may ourselves recall a time when we've opened ourselves to giving love one more try, we might imagine that Venus will have a change of heart. She's war's foil, after all. She's always had the propensity to be jealous or angry. Perhaps this explosion of negative emotion will lead her to let go of negativity, to reject the martial elements inside love. That certainly seems to be what Cupid is doing when he abandons his bow on the title page of a 1675 copy of Shakespeare's *Venus and Adonis* (Figure 2.2) located in the Folger Shakespeare Library archive.

The printer who published this now very-rare, pocket-sized edition of the poem opens the volume with this image as if to say that, after reading the poem, even the little love-god will put away weaponry and stop connecting love to war.

THE ENDS OF THINGS

Looking across Shakespeare's work, he does seem as vexed about the intersections of love and war as Venus is when the poem ends. In fact, Shakespeare at times seems to argue not only that less-desirable forms of love fuel war but also that war spreads varying forms of polluted love. The play *Troilus and Cressida*, for example, sets a doomed love story against the backdrop of the Trojan War. Pandarus, a character whose name is tied closely to the origins of our modern verb "to pander," acts as a matchmaker between the warrior Troilus and the young Cressida. It is all for his profit and does not do much for the Trojans' chances of beating the Greeks on the battlefield. Indeed, many of the heroes of Homer's epic poem, including Achilles and Patroclus, come off as petty in the play. *Troilus and Cressida* gives Pandarus the final speech. Consider this in comparison to the sentiments that end comedies

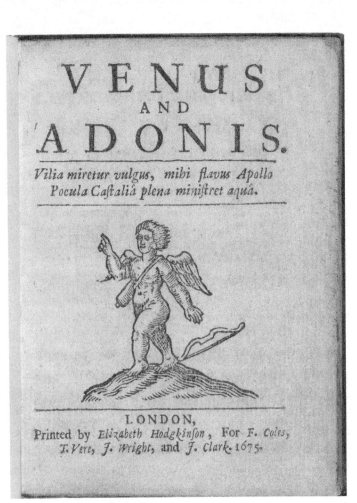

Figure 2.2 Love without the war (title page of *Venus and Adonis*, 1675, Folger Shakespeare Library)

such as *As You Like It* or *A Midsummer Night's Dream*. Pandarus tells the audience,

> A goodly medicine for my aching bones. O
> World, world, world! – thus is the poor agent despised.
> O traitors and bawds, how earnestly are you set a work,
> And how ill requited! why should our endeavour be so
> Desired and the performance so loathed? what verse
> For it? what instance for it? Let me see.
>
> (5.11.4–9)

He's complaining about his lot in life, but he's also admitting to being exactly those things that lose wars and cheapen love: a traitor and a pimp. He then goes on to tell the audience members that he recognizes that many of them are also bawds themselves:

> Good traders in the flesh, set this in your painted cloths.
> As many as be here of pander's hall,
> Your eyes, half out, weep out at Pander's fall.
> Or if you cannot weep, yet give some groans,
> Though not for me, yet for your aching bones.
>
> (5.11.14–18)

This is not Rosalind who recognizes fellow lovers in the audience and flirts with them. This is not Puck who likens the audience members to the lovers in the Athenian palace and enchants them with fairy dew. This is a pimp recognizing fellow pimps and observing that he shares bodily afflictions with them. Before he'll go, he uses one more device to insist that the audience members are just like him. In fact, he uses the language of family to do so, directly perverting the language of the "band of brothers" that was formed in the valorized war against France. But the audience isn't just composed of fellow members of Pandarus' profession. It seems they're even closer than that. The war, the pandering, and the play have infected them with his syphilis. Their own moaning and weeping at this performance are not loathing and laughter. They're symptoms of sexually transmitted disease:

> Brethren and sisters of the hold-door trade,
> Some two months hence my will shall here be made.
> It should be now, but that my fear is this.
> Some gallèd goose of Winchester would hiss.
> Till then I'll sweat and seek about for eases,
> And at that time bequeath you my diseases.
>
> (5.11.19–34)

We, as readers or audience members of the play, are told quite plainly: If you've enjoyed this play about the pernicious mixing of love and war, you're just as bad as any of them and should already be feeling symptoms of the disease with which seeing this play has infected you. In the doomed city of Troy, sex doesn't bring peace. When the Trojans are making love, they're making war. But their bad, diseased sex predicts that they will lose the war. For Pandarus, it doesn't seem there is a difference between the spoils of war and the spoils of sex. Both can soil you.

It is not necessarily an inconsistency across Shakespeare's work, however. He is making clear that there are different modes of loving, some successful and others not successful. He's inviting us to continually reconsider the challenge and the promise issued by the invitation to "Make Love, Not War."

LOVE FINDS A WAY

Peace-seeking audiences might long for the somewhat utopian scene that comes at the close of *Chi-Raq*, when Lysistrata and her lover, a gang-leader named Chi-Raq – a character standing in for the war zone itself – negotiate on top of a bed in an occupied armory. "What about peace?," she asks. "You're the only piece I need," he replies. The two end up breaking the sex strike, and the pun on "peace" as a gun, as sex, and as cessation of war finds fruition as gang members approach and toss their "pieces," their guns, onto the bed. Moments later, all the main characters, dressed in white, appear in the armory, where the bed has been replaced by a now-massive pile of guns (Figure 2.3).

Lysistrata proclaims, "Peace is not the absence of war, but a newfound love for one another." She announces that her lover no longer goes by the nickname "Chi-Raq" but rather has reverted to his given name "Demetrius," both humanizing him and linking him into a figure from the ancient Greek past. As he walks out of the scene, he implores others in the

Figure 2.3 All together now (*Chi-Raq*, Dir. Lee, Amazon Studios, 2015)

room and looks right into the camera: "Time for you to do the same. Take the blame. Take the claim. [. . .] Be a man and quit tryin' to suppress this pain you're in. Hell of a mess this gang you in."[22] It is a demand for new ways of being and new ways of relating.

We do not know if the fictional world of the film can realize sustainable peace. Peace Studies scholars argue that fantasies are crucial to determining how to reject the self-justification for warfare. Galtung writes that "imagination *has to* enter the process" for it is the only way "to account for the non-existing or not-yet-existing."[23] By giving us permission to return to and imagine past modes of expression as ones we might aspire toward, to ask how the seemingly private experience of love might speak to political concerns, to disrupt the binary distinction between spheres of social action and representations in the literary imagination, the as-yet unrealized promise of "Make Love, Not War" urges us to turn to the work of Shakespeare and other writers as compelling case studies through which to explore Galtung's claim.

NOTES

1 Aristophanes, *Lystistrata and Other Plays*, trans. Alan H. Sommerstein (New York: Penguin, 2008), line 799.

2 Johan Galtung, *Peace by Peaceful Means: Peace and Conflict, Development and Civilization* (London, Thousand Oaks, and New Delhi: SAGE Publications, 1996), 266.

3 See Melissa Sanchez, *Erotic Subjects, The Sexuality of Politics in Early Modern English Literature* (Oxford and New York: Oxford University Press, 2011), 3.

4 In a darker instance of the overlap between titillating sexual narratives and wartime, Galtung describes how bomber pilots in the Gulf War watched porn before leaving on missions to destroy military and civilian targets. Galtung, *Peace by Peaceful Means*, 42.

5 Some scholars believe that Fletcher and Shakespeare co-wrote *Henry VIII, The Two Noble Kinsmen*, and the lost play *Cardenio*.
6 He fears, however, that he will haunted by her ghost.
7 These plots that have women refuse sex to warring men of course over-simplify gender differences. We all know that not all men are built for war and that women can be just as aggressive as men. Aristophanes' audience would have known about the Amazons, for example. Still, recent research seems to reinforce major differences between women and men when it comes to predilections toward violence. Scientists have found that, while males of species might react to stressful situations with "fight-or-flight," females may have a tendency to "tend-and-befriend" in response to stress. Beth Azar, "A New Stress Paradigm for Women," *Monitor on Psychology* 31.7 (July/August 2000): 42.
8 In *Marie Claire*'s "The Future Is Female" issue in April 2017, artist Janelle Monáe called for a sex strike to advance gender equality, characterizing sex as "our power and our magic." On Twitter, she later clarified the statement to state that she did not mean to suggest sex as a "bargaining tool." Kevin Sessums, "Meet Our 2017 Fresh Faces," *Marie Claire* (April 10, 2017) and Janelle Monáe, Tweet, 6:45PM April 10, 2017.
9 The lines are quoted in Houston Wood, *Invitation to Peace Studies* (Oxford: Oxford University Press, 2015), 86.
10 "The Nobel Peace Prize for 2011," www.nobelprize.org/nobel_prizes/peace/laureates/2011/press.html
11 Leymah Gbowee, *Mighty Be Our Powers: How Sisterhood, Prayer, and Sex Changed a Nation at War* (New York: Beast Books, 2011), 148.
12 As we discussed in the introduction, theatrical performance and social activism are continually in dialogue with each other. In a nod to how fiction provides us with the stuff of real-world political action, Gene Sharp, founder of the Albert Einstein Institution (an organization dedicated to advancing the study of nonviolent action), calls sex strikes "Lysistratic nonaction." *Sharp's Dictionary of Power and Struggle: Language of Civil Resistance in Conflicts* (Oxford: Oxford University Press, 2011), 172.
13 Quoted in Dinesh D'Souza, *Ronald Reagan: How an Ordinary Man Became an Extraordinary Leader* (New York: Simon and Schuster, 1999), 71.
14 Hannah Arendt, *The Human Condition*, 2nd Edn., trans. Margaret Canovan (Chicago: University of Chicago Press, 1998), 242.

15 Michael Hardt, "For Love or Money," *Cultural Anthropology* 26.4 (November 2011): 677.

16 Sara Ahmed, *The Cultural Politics of Emotion* (London and New York: Routledge, 2014), 135.

17 Jasbir Puar, *Terrorist Assemblages: Homonationalism in Queer Times* (Durham: Duke University Press, 2007).

18 Lauren Berlant, "A Properly Political Concept of Love: Three Approaches in Ten Pages," *Cultural Anthropology* 26.4 (November 2011): 685.

19 Erasmus saw peace beginning in the home because "war is nothing else but a private quarrel extended to others." Desiderius Erasmus, "Dulce bellum inexpertis," in *The Adages of Erasmus*, trans. Margaret Mann Phillips (Cambridge: Cambridge University Press, 1964), 322. For a compelling argument that the connections within and between families lead to stronger, peace-enabling bonds at larger levels of community and nation, see Elaine Boulding, *Cultures of Peace* (Syracuse: Syracuse University Press, 2000).

20 Adam Phillips, *Unforbidden Pleasures* (New York: Farrar, Straus, and Giroux, 2016), 3.

21 A similar device was used in a 1947 production of *Twelfth Night* at the Shakespeare Memorial Theater in Stratford-Upon-Avon, which depicted Viola's matchmaking machinations as a way to heal relations fractured as a result of World War II. The production is described in Penny Gay, *As She Likes It: Shakespeare's Unruly Heroines* (London and New York: Routledge, 1994), 18–20.

22 Dolmedes, played by Samuel L. Jackson, ends the film by announcing: "The only real security is love y'all. L-O-V-E."

23 Galtung, *Peace by Peaceful Means*, 12.

Flower power
Three

The phrase "Flower Power" might call to mind Bernie Boston's 1967 photograph that captured a Vietnam War protester placing a carnation in the barrel of a Police Battalion member's rifle. Outside of its central action – one might even say metaphor – a part of what makes the photograph so striking is its larger framing. The protester wears a white, oversized knit sweater. The largely faceless battalion members wear helmets and dark uniforms, and seem almost entirely to surround the protester. The image remains interestingly ambiguous to this day. Is the scene spontaneous or meticulously staged? Are we supposed to imagine, just for a moment, that flowers are strong enough to deflect bullets? Is this a glance at another world with a new kind of rifle, one that fires flowers? Or does the image reinforce the cold consequences of rifles, the fragility of the protesters' bodies and, in turn, the inherent innocence and precarity of all human life? What makes this scene such a spectacle is that it asks us to hover on the cusp of possibility. It is the power of "if" that we saw to be so central to peace-making in Chapter One's description of *As You Like It*. The photograph asks, "What if the rifleman opens fire?" The opening credits of the science fiction film *Watchmen* (2009) give us a grim glimpse at the answer. A montage depicts a series of cultural milestones from the 1960s and

70s, including a peace protester placing her flower in the barrel of a national guardsman's rifle (Figure 3.1).

In the film's alternate history, the gesture is bitterly futile as the next thing we see is a round of gunshots in slow motion.[1] We witness what we have always feared – that the peace protester's actions will prove just as fragile and small as the flower itself.

Does Boston's image of the protester and the rifle distill the essence of Flower Power? That is, does this notion grasp our imaginations so firmly because it is so ephemeral, so strangely counter-intuitive? In the mockumentary *Spinal Tap*, a heavy metal band's hippie stage is exemplified by a performance of their song "Listen to the Flower People" (Figure 3.2).

The film describes the song as the group's first hit that allowed them "to tour the world, to tour the States," as one band member recollects. Another band member corrects him, "to tour the world and elsewhere." In front of a paisley backdrop with their message of "peace, love, and flower power," the band in their 1967 hit demands over and over in the

Figure 3.1 A precarious moment of "if" (*Watchmen*, Dir. Snyder, Warner Bros. Pictures, 2009)

Figure 3.2 Listen to what the flower people say (*This Is Spinal Tap*, Dir. Reiner, Spinal Tap Productions, 1984)

refrain that we listen to what the people say. Yet, intriguingly, the song never actually tells us *what* the flower people say.

In *Spinal Tap* and perhaps in the larger cultural imagination, Flower Power gets dismissed as a moment in time, a snapshot of a mood that has passed, a childhood phase, a form of psychedelic non-action, something that might be dreamed about by Timothy Leary with his often misunderstood "turn on, tune in, drop out" message.[2] But Flower Power *did* constitute a form of action, albeit a complex one. Poet Allen Ginsberg is often credited with coining the phrase "Flower Power" in a 1965 essay published in the *Berkeley Barb* and titled "Demonstration or Spectacle as Example, As Communication, or How to Make a March/Spectacle." However, he never actually uses the phrase in the article. It is more accurate to say that he conceived the notion and outlined its tactics.[3] Ginsberg's essay outlines ways to undermine in public the Hells Angels, who rallied in support of the Vietnam War and sometimes attacked protesters who favored peace.[4] To counter the motorcycle club and their occasionally violent tendencies, Ginsberg suggests a series of strategies that he characterizes as "imaginative, pragmatic, fun, gay, [and] happy."[5] Already, we can hear the comedic theatricality of his approach. It is full of contradiction, as imagination and play are foundations for the pragmatic. Indeed, Flower Power promises a gay old time at a war rally.

Ginsberg recommends that front-line demonstrators arm themselves with absurd weapons. They should carry crosses "like in the movies dealing with Dracula"; harmonicas, banjos, bongos, and tambourines; children's toys; candy bars; white flags; and finally "little paper halos" to present to the Hells Angels.[6] The promised force of Flower Power lies in its dramatization of "peace in action" or even how idleness is a form of waging peace. The crosses turn the dire seriousness of the pro-war contingent into movie monstrosity. The raucous music turns the protest into a festival. Toys emphasize the childish impulse to solve problems with guns. Candy bars ask us to be sweet to each other. White flags urge surrender rather than aggression, and the blank canvas of a white flag elides claims to shared identity that drive intergroup conflicts. Halos remind the Hells Angels of the better side of their natures (and redirect our attention to the second half of their group's name). Ginsberg's suite of tactics emphasizes that to give peace a chance requires us to rethink and suspend our assumptions.

At the heart of its strategies, Flower Power encourages play and performance. It is interesting to compare Ginsberg's list of tactics to that of Peace Studies scholar Gene Sharp, who researched and catalogued 198 methods in his seminal work on nonviolent action. In Sharp's "198 Methods of Nonviolent Action," only three methods appear under the heading "Drama and Music." These are "humorous skits and pranks," "performances of plays and music," and "singing."[7] Ginsberg's vision for Flower Power encourages us to see a much more expansive overlap between drama and nonviolent action. If we look at other items on Sharp's list such as "mock funerals," "mock awards," "rude gestures," "symbolic lights," "wearing of symbols," and "protest disrobings," we can begin to see how his widely adopted modes of resistance resonate as highly theatrical. That is, peace protest tactics might be more theatrical than Sharp imagines.

Here's where Shakespeare comes in.

THE TRIUMPH OF PEACE

Consider this thought experiment: Imagine the fairies of *A Midsummer Night's Dream* (1600) as "flower children." Ginsberg describes his mischievous peace protesters as a "corps of trained fairies." And the link between fairies and pacifism abides today. Kate Bornstein, for example, lists 21st-century "radical faeries" among those groups central to her vision for the peace movement articulated in the workbook *A Step-by-Step Guide to Achieving World Peace Through Gender Anarchy and Sex Positivity*.[8] What if we place Shakespeare's fairy folk in this emergent genealogy of peacemakers? The mystical inhabitants of the forest outside Athens certainly advocate free love, play games, and use mind-altering potions. The play's human characters, too, seem prone to childish antics as they swoon and moon excessively over lovers, all in spite of the members of an older, warmongering generation from whom they escape into the forest. The schemes of the fairy folk and the frantic action of the human lovers dramatize how "peace is more than the absence of war" in the words of Peace Studies scholar Thomas Gregor.[9] In fact, *A Midsummer Night's Dream* opens just after a period of war. Athens has emerged victorious in a final battle with the Amazons, and Theseus, the Duke of Athens, has captured Hippolyta, the Queen of the Amazons. In the opening scene of Shakespeare's play, Theseus reminisces to his new beloved:

> Hippolyta, I wooed thee with my sword,
> And won thy love doing thee injuries.
> But I will wed thee in another key –
> With pomp, with triumph, and with reveling.
> (1.1.16–19)

In the previous chapter, we saw Mars ready to trade battlefield aggression for courtly behavior. Here, too, we see a Theseus ready to try a new way of being in the spirit of love-making and peace-making. Here, once more, we see love and war as complex foils when Theseus' sword functions as a weapon for killing and a tool for wooing. When they were physical combatants on opposite sides, Theseus did Hippolyta "injuries." War-making was foreplay to love-making as the couple *made war in order to make love*. In this, we hear echoes of how in Shakespeare's time (and in our own), "*la petite mort*" (the little death) was a favored French phrase to describe an orgasm. In our own contemporary military slang, "no joy" declares that a pilot was unable to acquire a target either visually or on radar. It seems at first that in *A Midsummer Night's Dream*, love is once more a battlefield. After setting its scene, however, this play seems to reject the notion that love and war must be yoked to each other. Instead, it posits that romantic desire – even if driven by fantasy – is a means toward lasting, peaceful reconciliation. The entertainments of *A Midsummer Night's Dream* and other comedies display a desirable world much preferable to the strife and scarcity of wartime, helping us understand why the Utopians described in Thomas More's *Utopia* (1516) considered "nothing so much against glory as glory gotten in war."[10] Shakespearean comedy, as our study has begun to show, suggests that glory is possible in peacetime when we conceive of new forms of glory made possible by idle play.

Just as Shakespeare understood love and war to have a more complicated relationship than that of opposites, he knew the same to be true of peace and war. Such thinking runs counter to more simplistic arguments that circulated during the early modern period. Take, for example, Barnabe Rich's *The Fruits of Long Experience: A Pleasing View for Peace, a Looking Glass for War* (1604). The book's title immediately implies the inextricability of peace and war by describing them as mirrored twins. The volume depicts two captains in dialogue with each other, as one articulates a version of the just war argument when he asserts, "war is to be undertaken but to the end to have peace [because] the laws of nation and the laws of nature both admit it."[11] In *The Arte of English Poesy* (1589), George Puttenham reiterates the logic that peace and war are both necessary states that feed each other. He quotes French poet Jean de Meun:

Peace makes plenty, and plenty makes pride;
Peace brings quarrel, and quarrel brings war
[. . .]
So peace brings war, and war brings peace.[12]

In *Solace for the Soldier and Sailor* (1592), Simon Harward warns, "Peace has increased plenty, plenty has wrought pride, pride has hatched disdain, and disdain has brought forth such strife and debates, such suits of law, such quarrelling and contentions, as never heard in any age before us."[13] These writers share a belief in the cyclical nature of war and peace, where the drive to build nations, bolster pride, and realize economic gain motivates humankind to alternating states of discord and harmony. Such examples make visible the strand of thought that Ben Lowe has traced in the period leading up to the birth of Shakespeare, a line of thinking notably subtended by a "common syllogism that depicted war and peace as turns in a perpetual and inescapable cycle to which all people need be resigned."[14] However, he notes that this began to change toward the end of the 16th century as "many Elizabethans challenged this hardened, deterministic outlook, and their humanist sensibilities denied such inevitability."[15]

Comedies such as *A Midsummer Night's Dream* may very well fit in this new mode of thinking that sought to break the cycle of inevitable military conflict. Arundhati Roy has remarked, "People rarely win wars, governments rarely lose them." She adds, "People get killed. Governments moult and re-group, hydra-headed."[16] These claims throw into relief the nationalistic drive toward conflict and the ways in which cyclical logics anonymize human actors in the theater of war. Contemporary peace theorists tell us that war is hero-less, rejecting the long-standing logic that "true heroism" stems from "the kind of selfless act that only occurs within the military setting."[17] Fictional narratives, including Shakespeare's plays, can showcase individual characters who help us identify unheroic protagonists at the center of wars and heroic protagonists in peacetime.

In order to transition from the action of war to the action of peace, Shakespeare's play uses its warrior-king Theseus as connective tissue. The violence of the Amazonian conflict was prelude not only to conjugal attachment between combatants but also to theatrical performance in the Athenian court. Theseus describes his and Hippolyta's impending wedding celebration as a "triumph," a term in Shakespeare's time which meant *both* "victory" or "conquest" *and* "spectacle." Writing in 1625, Francis Bacon describes "triumphs" as elaborate courtly performances, as "toys" whose characters should include "sprites," "antics," "nymphs," and "rustics."[18] Theseus' promise of a grand performance characterized by "triumph" intermingles love and war while also setting the stage for the spectacle that Shakespeare's audience is about to view. When playgoers hear that nymphs and sprites armed with toys will inhabit the stage, it would be unclear whether Theseus describes the court spectacle planned for his wedding day or the forthcoming fairy mischief in the forest. Early moderns were aware of the intriguing contradictions in the term "triumph" and how it could be connected to pacifist impulses. For example, an elaborate 1634 court masque by James Shirley combines the two terms in its title, *The Triumph of Peace*, and has personifications of Peace, Justice, and Law honor King Charles I. With the toy-wielding fairies of Ginsberg's essay in mind, we ourselves might see the terms of early modern "triumph" applying just as well to a peace protest at U.C. Berkeley.

IDLE THEMES AND PACIFIST DREAMS

The major conflict of the play starts when an elder of Athens named Egeus attempts to force a marriage upon his daughter Hermia. If she will not concede to her father's demand to wed Demetrius, she must accept either death or life-long chastity as a devotee of the goddess Diana. However, she would rather wed rival suitor Lysander. Like other characters we've encountered in our study, Lysander sees love as a battlefield. Complaining to Hermia, he says,

> If there were a sympathy in choice,
> War, death, or sickness did lay siege to it,
> Making it momentary as a sound,
> Swift as a shadow, short as any dream,
> Brief as the lightning in the collied night
> (1.1.141–145)

For Theseus, war was preamble to love. Yet for Lysander, war dissuades love. War eliminates the luxury of choice since the time necessary for sound decisions is available only during times of peace – or times of "plenty" as Puttenham and Harard both described it earlier.[19] If peacetime is often all too brief to cultivate love, comedy gives us the time needed to take a breath, to see what might happen. Lysander adds this about war's threat to choice: "The jaws of darkness do devour it up./So quick bright things come to confusion" (1.1.148–149). War confuses the path of love and confuses the focus of lovers, as the "quick bright things" in the final line could stand in for love affairs and for the lovers themselves. With Hermia and Lysander in love, Demetrius in love with Hermia, and Helena in love with Demetrius, the young lovers' only recourse is to escape by fleeing to a place where "sharp Athenian law/Cannot pursue us" (1.1.164–165). In this comedy whose opening scene coincides with the start of peacetime, the plot promises plenty of conflict here and plenty of action.

Outside Athens, Oberon is "passing fell and wrath," furious because the Fairy Queen Titania has stolen away an Indian boy of whom he is fond (2.1.20). Here, where there is only one child, a boy whom each of them desires, the lack of *plenty* signals a paucity of *peace*. An economy of scarcity drives conflict, as Oberon promises Titania, "Thou shalt not from this grove/ Till I torment thee for this injury" (2.1.146–147). When we last heard the term "injury," Theseus was describing his battlefield wooing of Hippolyta, where skirmish was prelude to reconciliation and love. Here, the "injury" is purely psychic as Titania has taken away an object that Oberon loves. As Shankar Raman observes, their contest over possession of the child can be likened to English desires for commodities from the East such that "the Indian Boy's transfer ties the domestic unit to the emergence of the market."[20] The movement of the boy from the East to the West (ancient Athens in the play, Renaissance England in the theater) links the "family" of Titania and Oberon to the practice of colonialism and to the origins of the conflict between the Amazons and Athens. That war began as retaliation for Theseus carrying off Antiope, the sister of Hippolyta. Both the earlier conflict and the current conflict derive from an economy of scarcity – a situation where there is not enough to go around – and this links the fairy and the human monarchs to the young lovers who can't allocate love correctly between them. David Marshall observes, "throughout the play, characters are figured as merchandise or stolen goods."[21] Yet the playgoers can see what is obvious: *There in fact is plenty to go around.* Oberon and Titania might raise the child together, and the four human lovers could just re-align themselves so that each has a desired partner. These characters just need to open themselves to the power of "if." Concluding the play will entail a form of ordering and the assurance of the "plenty" necessary for peace. And this plenty will be made possible by the power of a flower.

Realizing a means to resolve his conflict with Titania, Oberon recalls for Puck that once he spied "Cupid, all armed" (2.1.157). He continues:

> A certain aim he took
> At a fair vestal thronèd by the west,
> And loosed his love-shaft smartly from his bow
> As it should pierce a hundred thousand hearts.
> (2.1.157–160)

This description of the mischievous boy-god invokes themes we have seen before. Love is associated with abundance (the "hundred thousand hearts"), and Cupid's bow and arrow (his "love-shaft") frame romantic desire as a mode of martial play. Archery occupies the same role as Theseus' swordplay with Hippolyta that resulted in her capitulation to be his wife. Oberon continues:

> Yet marked I where the bolt of Cupid fell.
> It fell upon a little western flower –
> Before, milk-white: now purple with love's wound –
> And maidens call it love-in-idleness.
> (2.1.165–168)

Once more, we find ourselves confronted by the injury of love, here where "love's wound" conflates pain and desire. The flower's power is to engender romantic desire and to compel those afflicted with the flower's nectar to act upon that desire. Because of the "flower's force in stirring love," Titania will fall in love with Bottom (a man with the head of an ass), while Demetrius and Lysander both will fall in love with Helena (2.2.75). These represent choices that will cause conflict, but the play's overt status as a comedy lets us know that these choices can be revoked and reconsidered. The name of the wounded flower, "love-in-idleness," reminds us that peace, love, and understanding are possible only when we pause and give ourselves to the opportunity to find pleasure in times of stasis.

The effect of the flower is fairy magic, but it is also stage magic. In some sense, we know the characters are acting. What they profess to experience may feel real, but it is not. They are under a spell, meaning that they are people just pretending to be in love. Madhavi Menon suggests, "Posing insistently the question of what causes desire and how we recognize it, *A Midsummer Night's Dream* suggests daringly that desire might not produce an identity we can use as the basis for subjectivity."[22] Put another way, we are all actors when it comes to love. Desire doesn't tell us whom we are deep down; it creates new identities for us that are always subject to change. In Shakespeare's play, two lovers feud over a young boy whom we never see. Four lovers fawn over each other, though we know half of them act on motivations that are not heartfelt. Another dose of an herbal antidote will bring some of the characters back to their senses, but they will all be transformed by the experience. The flower-fueled love games in the play have dramatized how a shift in perspective can change what we desire and how we act. Erasmus believed that "external peace" was possible only once one obtained "inner peace" because one must first establish that which "calms him and soothes him and frees him from all anxiety, horror, fear, and disturbing thoughts."[23] It is only from this starting point of the transformed self that one can begin to dream that another world is possible. The spectacle of the drama in the forest, all taking place before the "triumph" that Theseus has promised at his wedding, has peace-making force for participants and onlookers alike.

This play's dynamic where fantasy and love combine to spur individuals toward re-imagining the world is shared by the anti-war elements at the heart of the 1960s notion of Flower Power. In 1967, Abbie Hoffman warned pro-war factions, "Plans are being made to mine the East River with daffodils. Dandelion chains are being wrapped around induction centers."[24] The use of "mine" and "chains" emphasizes how the spectacle transforms flowers into exactly what they are not: explosive, deadly, hard, and prohibitive. These counter-intuitive claims about flowers, in turn, throw into relief the *unnaturalness* of war. We hear the name of something that is, in fact, meant to grow out of the ground (flowers) rather than be placed in it (landmines). "Induction" is a term meaning not only to initiate or bring about but also to engage in a form of reasoning that might reveal unexpected conclusions. Instead of entering centers designed to convert drafted civilians into soldiers, onlookers are blocked out by the flimsiest of barriers. Would-be-warriors are arrested by fleeting beauty and are urged to consider peaceful alternatives. Hoffman adds, "The cry of 'Flower Power' echoes through the land. We shall not wilt." We realize here that, while flowers are the unlikely weapons of the activist, the activists themselves too are flowers. Members of the New York Workshop in Nonviolence went as far as to announce that Armed Forces Day would in the future be re-named "Flower Power Day."[25] The whole point is to make us pause, rethink our assumptions, and overcome our passivity.

Casting Shakespeare's play in the light of Flower Power helps us see the absurdity of the idea that flowers might resolve political conflict while firmly demanding that we accept this possibility. Yet the connection between the play and the social movement also suggests a shared line of thinking that can grant new insight into the operations of peaceful reconciliation. With all seriousness, Hoffman describes flowers as the unlikely weapons of the activist and represents the activists themselves as flowers. The idea finds a surprising antecedent in the 1614 *Masque of Flowers*, an elaborate courtly performance presented by Francis Bacon at the wedding of the Earl and Countess of Somerset. While overtly framed as a wedding triumph much like that of Theseus and Hippolyta, the masque has clear political overtones. The performance culminated with members of James' court dressed as flowers and offering themselves to the king, each one kissing his hand and swearing fealty. As odd as this drama might seem, it falls within the logic of the other instances of Flower Power that we see in *A Midsummer Night's Dream* and in the 1960s activism. Bacon, Ginsberg, Hoffman, and Shakespeare seem to share a belief that flowers and theater can combine to make us pause, rethink our assumptions, and give peace a chance.[26] The more compelling the theater, the more likely that onlookers will find its messages infectious. The more startling and counter-intuitive its spectacles, the more likely they are to engage audiences' imaginations. This seems as true for pacifist street theater as for the action in Shakespeare's Globe Theater. In fact, the final act of *A Midsummer Night's Dream* makes explicit what scholars of early modern performance have increasingly urged us to see: "the audience as a partner in the production of meaning on the [. . .] stage."[27]

PEACE AS LAUGHABLE PERFORMANCE

By the time we arrive at the wedding of Theseus and Hippolyta, most audience members probably feel like the action has all wrapped up. A new flower potion has been applied to resolve the conflicts of the human love quadrangle and of Titania's lust for the transformed Bottom. Lysander and Hermia can be together. Demetrius and Helena are now in love with each other. Oberon and Titania are reconciled. Bottom is back to being human. Well, perhaps not entirely human. He still shows signs of exposure to the power of the magic flower in his complexion. His face now has a "cherry nose" with "yellow cowslip cheeks," and his "eyes were green as leeks" (5.1.348–352). We still see a touch of the fairy world in his face, and perhaps he sees the human world as brimming with fairy possibilities, too. The play winds toward its final moments as the humans gather at the palace back in Athens. Learning about the strange goings-on in the forest, Theseus rationalizes the fantasies that had gripped the young lovers:

> Such tricks hath strong imagination
> That if it would but apprehend some joy,
> It comprehends some bringer of that joy;
> Or in the night, imagining some fear,
> How easy is a bush supposed a bear!
> (5.1.18–22)

His comments call attention to the role of choice in determining our reactions. When someone wants to feel happiness, the imagination will bring the cause into being. The mind must be trained to look for joy in order to see good in the world. It is only from this starting point of the transformed self that one can begin to dream that another world is possible.

But Shakespeare isn't quite finished; he still has to give us the final act. *Pyramus and Thisbe* – the main action of the conclusion – is not exactly guerrilla theater designed to bring about political change. It is decidedly bad and done for laughs, both for the audience at the wedding and the audience of *A Midsummer Night's Dream*. The short play performed by Bottom and his fellow actors seems to be the "triumph" that Theseus promised his bride at the start of the play. Before the show, Lysander reads the program: "A tedious brief scene of young Pyramus/And his love Thisbe: very tragical mirth" (5.1.56–57). The summary is full of contradictions, pinpointed by its "tedious" brevity and "tragical" joy.[28] These incongruences do not go unnoticed as Theseus reacts to the summary of the play:

> "Merry" *and* "tragical?" "Tedious" *and* "brief?"
> That is, hot ice and wondrous strange black snow.
> How shall we find the concord of this discord?
> (5.1.58–60)

The court "triumph" sounds like a confused dream, but its summary does seem to track closely to the antics that have pervaded the play overall. The pursuit of love offers an endeavor where conflict, differences of opinion, and reversals can all sit comfortably. *A Midsummer Night's Dream* is, after all, the play from which we have the phrase "the course of true love never did run smooth" (1.1.134). The truer the love, the more error-filled its path to full realization. Confusion and contradiction abound, threatening the "concord" into which we expect any drama to resolve. As Matthew Steggle notes, the breakdown between emotional states promised by the court performance is "partially recuperated by Theseus' awareness of the wider social functions of the performance of *Pyramus and Thisbe*, and by Puck's framing dialogue."[29] That is, the "tragical mirth" of *Pyramus and Thisbe* erodes the distinction between an audience's propensities for laughing and crying in such a way as to predict how Puck's epilogue will break down the distinction between the emotions performed by the actors and the emotions that the audience members will carry inside them from the theater.

Pyramus and Thisbe tells the story of lovers who escape to the forest for a rendezvous. Rather than resolving in the happy ending of *A Midsummer Night's Dream*, these lovers' adventure ends tragically more in line with *Romeo and Juliet*. One lover falsely believes the other dead and so kills herself. In finding his dead lover, the other takes his own life. Like the alternate history where the rifle opens fire in the opening credits of *Watchmen*, the performance displays a darker version of the events of *A Midsummer Night's Dream*. Both *Pyramus and Thisbe* and *Watchmen* urge audiences to consider the negative power of "if," and in doing so urge them to maintain a less dangerous world where the law allows love to be chosen freely and peace maintained.

When the wedding entertainment ends, all the human characters rush off to bed. Perhaps the unfortunate end of *Pyramus and Thisbe* has made them want to seize the moment for their own happy endings. In the penultimate speech of *A Midsummer Night's Dream*, just before Puck's farewell to the audience, Oberon bids his fairies to leave a bit of the forest magic within the courtly world:

> With this field-dew consecrate
> Every fairy take his gait
> And each several chamber bless
> Through this palace with sweet peace.
> (5.2.45–48)

Another kind of love potion, another touch of flowers perhaps in this "field-dew," will now be applied to the sleeping lovers and, by extension, the audience members too. This is what Flower Power promises: that the green world of nature might temper the hard edges of the city, that the theater informs the political sphere, that confounding paradoxes might occupy our minds more compellingly than simplistic, violent thoughts. Relocating the youthful lovers back into the city also carries the promise of safety. Unlike in the beginning of the play when the city was still under the shadow of war and threatened death for disobedient children, Athens now appears gentle and welcoming.

THE CITY, NOT LONG AFTER

In the epilogue to *A Midsummer Night's Dream*, the spritely Puck comes on stage to suggest that everything in the forest and the court was simply a dream, an "idle theme" (E.4). On the one hand, that dismissal allows Shakespeare's audiences to deny the troubling elements of the drama they have just witnessed, since it is not worth getting upset at a frivolous entertainment. On the other hand, Puck's epilogue allows idealism to obtain purchase on the human world. Before he leaves the stage, Puck requests that "we be friends," an agreement that depends upon our recognizing parity across the fairy court, the forest, and the Athenian court as well as between the audience, the characters, and the actors. It is an invitation, like Rosalind's final speech in *As You Like It*, that requires buy-in from audiences or, as Alison Hopgood puts nicely, "imagining [playgoers] not as disciplined receivers of dramatic passions but rather as potent and productive co-creators of the drama they attended."[30] The power of "love-in-idleness" has been to resolve conflicts within the human world – between the human lovers and by extension between parents and their children – and between members of the fairy world. In fact, we can extend the reach of *A Midsummer Night's Dream*'s resolution even further when we acknowledge that play endings constitute thresholds where actors meet audiences. While a classic formulation of Shakespearean theater argues that the stage operates as a site of containment, we see that peace pervades the audience and the courtly world here in this play. As Amanda Bailey and Mario DiGangi write early modern playgoers experienced a play as "an event that immersed them in experience of the transmissibility and translatability of affect between and among players and audience members."[31] The audience is caught in the spell, invited to project their own imagination to generate the *real* of the *fantasy*. Oberon's call at the end for Puck to spread mystical field-dew throughout the palace for "sweet peace" urges the audience to take with them what they've felt, rather than to leave it behind.[32]

Puck tells the audience they have just experienced the play as a shared dream. This closing speech tells the audience that "all is mended" and three times repeats the word "amends," emphasizing not only that the torn political and romantic order has been restored, in our contemporary sense of this word, but also that everyone – even the playgoers – has undergone personal reformations in the early modern sense of "mend." Indeed, "mend" and "amends" both derive from the Latin *emendo, emendare*, which means to free someone from faults. Here, in perhaps Shakespeare's most well-known comedy, love forgives everyone for their previous errors. It heals a family beset by patriarchal tension, agitated monarchs dueling over possession, rival nations, and the playgoers themselves, whether they knew they needed that healing or not. Either in the form of courtly theater or of recent anti-war protests, peacetime actions such as these provide a proofpoint for R. S. White's claim that "where voices of war are raised they inevitably provoke, and are sometimes defeated by, equally powerful voices of peace."[33] Shakespearean comedy suggests that glory is possible in peacetime when we conceive of new forms of active, conflict-resolving work made possible by idleness. With this in mind, the fairy king Oberon's promise that "all things shall be peace" (3.2.378) by the end of the play has real political implications inseparable from the romantic play that will dominate the narrative. The peace movement's slogans "Make Love, Not War" and "Flower Power" surprisingly find expression and intertwine in *A Midsummer Night's Dream* as the play positions lovers' antics and fairy play not as dismissible fancies but rather as real strategies for channeling social restlessness into a new narrative.[34]

This chapter's thought experiment, where we imagined the characters of Shakespeare's play to be flower children, suggests how comedic drama can position love as a driver of peaceable outcomes and how it imagines those outcomes to be sustainable. About the 1960s peace movement, Michael Kramer remarks,

> the flowering of flower power in the counterculture was never just the naïve blossoming of a simplistic ideology of peace and love [. . .] it was something more [. . .] an efflorescence of civic engagement that continues to matter because the need remains to invent modes of citizenship suitable for the difficult conditions of more recent times.[35]

We hear in this assessment of Flower Power similar ideas as expressed by scholars who consider the ending of *A Midsummer Night's Dream*. Neither the movement nor the play truly ends, and both shape the future of those exposed. Tanya Pollard nicely describes the variety of outcomes possible for audience members who have witnessed the drug-induced antics of Shakespeare's play: "All of these lovers are firmly identified with the play's external audience; not only because of the shared act of watching a play, but especially because of Puck's description, in the epilogue, of the audience of sleepers who have dreamed the play."[36] Pollard notes that different characters have been changed in different ways – Lysander is returned to his former state when given an antidote, Demetrius is left permanently in drug-induced love, and Titania has been "returned and altered" – and that each of these outcomes is possible for a playgoer having seen the play.[37] Indeed, such outcomes remain open possibilities for future audiences as well.[38]

NOTES

1 To emphasize how our history could have gone the way of the film's, the opening montage is presented accompanied by Bob Dylan's "The Time's They Are A-Changing."

2 Leary later changed it to "drop in." He was also one of the friends who recorded "Give Peace a Chance" with John Lennon and Yoko Ono, and he is mentioned in the final stanza of the song.

3 For instances where he is credited with coining the term in the 1965 Berkeley Barb essay (where it does not appear), see Tony Perry, "Poet Allen Ginsberg Dies at 70," *Los Angeles Times* (April 6, 1997) and the "Guide to the Allen Ginsberg Papers: Biography/Administrative History," in *The Online Archive of California* (Palo Alto: Stanford University, 1997), 3. cdn.calisphere.org/data/13030/hb/tf5c6004hb/files/tf5c6004hb.pdf. Abbie Hoffman does use the phrase "Flower Power" to describe the cry of the peace movement in a 1967 essay in *WIN Magazine*. Quoted in Marty Jezer, *Abbie Hoffman: American Rebel* (New Brunswick: Rutgers University Press, 1993), 108.

4 "Hells Angels Attack Peace March at UC," *Los Angeles Times* (October 17, 1965), 1.

5 Allen Ginsberg, "Demonstration or Spectacle as Example, As Communication, or How to Make a March/Spectacle," *Berkeley Barb* (November 19, 1965), republished in *The Portable Sixties Reader*, ed. Ann Charles (New York: Penguin, 2002), 208.

6 Ginsberg, "Demonstration or Spectacle," 208.
7 Gene Sharp, *There Are Realistic Alternatives* (Boston: The Albert Einstein Institution, 2003), 40.
8 Kate Bornstein, *My New Gender Workbook: A Step-By-Step Guide to Achieving World Peace Through Gender Anarchy and Sex Positivity*, 2nd Edn. (London and New York: Routledge, 2013), 179.
9 Thomas Gregor, "Introduction," in *A Natural History of Peace*, ed. Thomas Gregor (Nashville: Vanderbilt University Press, 1996), xiv.
10 Thomas More, *Utopia*, trans. Ralph Robinson (Oxford: Oxford University Press 1999), 97.
11 Barnabe Rich, *The Fruites of Long Experience a Pleasing View for Peace, a Looking-Glasse for Warre, or, Call It What You List: Discoursed Betweene Two Captaines* (London: Thomas Creede for Jeffrey Chorlton, 1604), B2r.
12 George Puttenham, *The Art of Enligh Poesy, Critical Edition*, ed. Frank Whigham and Wayne A. Rebhorn (Ithaca: Cornell University Press, 2007), 293.
13 Simon Harward, *Solace for the Soldier and Sailor* (London: Thomas Orwin for Thomas Wight, 1592), B3v.
14 Ben Lowe, *Imagining Peace: A History of Early English Pacifist Ideas, 1340–1560* (University Park: The Pennsylvania State University Press, 1997), 302.
15 Lowe, *Imagining Peace*, 302.
16 Arundhati Roy, "War is peace," in *The Power of Nonviolence: Writings by Advocates of Peace*, ed. Howard Zinn (Boston: Beacon Press, 2002), 183.
17 Jacqueline Haessly, "A hero for the twenty-first century," *Peace Studies, Public Policy, and Global Security*, Vol. III, ed. Ursula Oswald Spring, Ada Aharoni, Ralph V. Summy, Robert Charles Elliot (Oxford: EOLSS Publishers/UNESCO, 2010), 63.
18 Francis Bacon, "Of masques and triumphs," in *Francis Bacon: The Major Works*, ed. Brian Vickers (Oxford: Oxford University Press, 2002), 416–17.
19 In yet another example of the Renaissance association of plenty with peace, Marston's *Histrio-Mastix* has the character Peace lead the character Plenty onto the stage. John Marston, *Histrio-Mastix, or, the Player Whipt* (London: Thorp, 1610).
20 Shakar Raman, *Framing 'India': The Colonial Imaginary in Early Modern Culture* (Palo Alto: Stanford University Press, 2002), 278–9.
21 David Marshall, "Exchanging Visions: Reading a Midsummer Night's Dream" *ELH* 49.3 (Autumn 1982): 568.

22 Madhavi Menon, "Desire," in *Early Modern Theatricality*, ed. Henry S. Turner (Oxford: Oxford University Press, 2014), 343.

23 Desiderius Erasmus, *De Contemptu Mundi* in *Collected Works of Erasmus*, ed. John W. O'Malley and trans. Erika Rummel (Toronto: University of Toronto Press, 1988), Book 5, Sec. 1255B, 162.

24 The lines appeared in the June 16, 1967, issue of *Win: A Publication of the New York Workshop in Nonviolence*. Quoted in Marty Jezer, *Abbie Hoffman: American Rebel* (New Brunswick: Rutgers University Press, 1993), 105.

25 Jezer, *Abbie Hoffman*, 105.

26 Perhaps this is the larger point of so many of the odd and hyperbolic actions by peace activists. Leyhah Gbowee, for example, has said that the point of the Liberian sex strike was to get people to listen. Gbowee remarks that the point of the women's actions "was for us to get the attention of the men in Liberia, to say even if you are not a fighter, you have a dear buddy that is a fighter that you need to talk to because he needs to see reason to end the war." Ebong Udoma, "Interview: Leymah Gbowee, The Nobel Laureate Who Helped End Liberia's Civil War," *WSHU Public Radio*, April 24, 2017, http://wshu.org/post/interview-leymah-gbowee-nobel-laureate-who-helped-end-liberia-s-civil-war

27 Nova Myhill and Jennifer A. Low, "Introduction: Audience and audiences," in *Imagining the Audience in Early Modern Drama, 1558–1642*, ed. Nova Myhill and Jennifer A. Low (New York: Palgrave Macmillan, 2011), 10.

28 The phrase "tragical mirth" resembles Claudius' language in the first act of *Hamlet*. He describes himself and Gertrude being "With mirth in funeral and with dirge in marriage,/In equal scale weighing delight and dole" (1.2.12–13). His description of love is not divorced from issues of war. He describes Gertrude as "our sometime sister, now our queen,/Th' imperial jointress to this warlike state" (1.2.8–9). Of course, we know that his marriage won't settle the warlike state – far from it, in fact.

29 Matthew Steggle, *Laughing and Weeping in Early Modern Theatres* (Aldershot and Burlington: Ashgate, 2007), 198.

30 Alison P. Hopgood, *Passionate Playgoing in Early Modern England* (Cambridge: Cambridge University Press, 2014), 28.

31 Amanda Bailey and Mario DiGangi, "Introduction," in *Affect Theory and Early Modern Texts: Politics, Ecologies, and Form*, ed. Amanda Bailey and Mario DiGangi (New York: Palgrave Macmillan, 2017), 16.

32 By placing the events of the play in the distant past, as many of the comedies featured in our study do, Shakespeare contributes to the project where "theatrical performance offered a way to bring alternative forms of civil society to mind, to reimagine community, and, as a consequence, to crystallize new powers of critical, embodied social thought into historical actuality." Steven Mullaney, *The Reformation of Emotions in the Age of Shakespeare* (Chicago and London: University of Chicago Press, 2015), 167.

33 R. S. White, *Pacifism and English Literature: Minstrels of Peace* (New York: Palgrave Macmillan, 2008), 177.

34 Seventeenth-century diarist Samuel Pepys saw the play performed in 1662 and described it as "the most insipid ridiculous play that ever I saw performed in my life." Fair enough. But maybe that's the point. Samuel Pepys, *The Diary of Samuel Pepys*, ed. Richard Le Gallienne (New York: The Modern Library, 2003), 74.

35 Michael J. Kramer, *The Republic of Rock: Music and Citizenship in the Sixties Counterculture* (Oxford: Oxford University Press, 2017), 22.

36 Tanya Pollard, *Drugs and Theatre in Early Modern England* (Oxford: Oxford University Press, 2005), 146.

37 Pollard, *Drugs and Theatre*, 146.

38 One of the more intriguing contemporary adaptations of the play is *The Donkey Show: A Midsummer Night's Disco*. The adaptation was conceived in 1999 by husband and wife creative team Diane Paulus and Randy Weiner, first opening for only a six-week limited engagement at an actual dance venue, Club El Flamingo, on August 18, 1999, and ultimately running for six years Off Broadway. The disco setting showcases a love quadrangle among four characters who take party drugs and dance to 70s hit songs such as "I Will Survive," "Carwash," "We Are Family," "Don't Leave Me This Way," and "You Sexy Thing." As a *New York Times* review describes, "Slowly the cast members, who have been mingling with the audience (the men wear little more than spandex briefs), evolve into characters, and we're gradually drawn into the whirlwind farce of Shakespeare's confused lovers." The experience of watching the play and performing as part of the play is blurred, and its memorable songs combine with Shakespeare's familiar language to open the possibility that the spirit of the performance will carry into the real world after the show. Peter Marks, "They Be Foolish Mortals Who Love the Nightlife," *New York Times* (August 27, 1999).

Blowin' in the wind
Four

Bob Dylan's "Blowin' in the Wind" holds a curious place in the pantheon of protest songs. Most obviously, the author denies that it is a protest song. Even though Sam Cooke may take inspiration in writing "A Change Is Gonna Come," and even though anti-war activists may continue to sing "Blowin' in the Wind" at rallies, they do so in defiance of Dylan himself. "This here ain't a protest song or anything like that, 'cause I don't write protest songs," Dylan said in 1962. "I'm just writing it as something to be said, for somebody, by somebody."[1] Dylan often courts such ambiguity, and his claim to write "something to be said" hardly illuminates anything. In another exposé, he offered this non-explanation: "There ain't too much I can say about this song except the answer is blowing in the wind."[2] You could come to that same conclusion in just listening to the song. In fact, "Blowin' in the Wind" dares its audience to try and sort out the answers. Dylan famously asks, "how many?" – including "how many times must the cannon balls fly/before they're forever banned?" – as the refrain repeatedly answers, "the answer, my friend, is blowin' in the wind/the answer is blowin' in the wind."[3] If you try to count the number of roads or cannon balls, you miss the point. That sort of quantification can provide one particular truth or reality, but it doesn't give an explanation. Counting won't resolve the fundamental ambiguity or confusion at the heart of Dylan's view.

In the same interview that denies "Blowin' in the Wind" an explanation, Dylan continues, "I still say that some of the biggest criminals are those that turn their heads away when they see wrong and know it's wrong. I'm only 21 years old I know there's been too many wars."[4] The song, in other words, speaks to the peace movement but isn't a protest song. That inconclusiveness might just be what makes the song so effective. In the face of "realism" and "hard truth," it gives vague and open-ended questions. Wind can be measured, but it will not itself give numbers.

In this chapter, we follow that notion into visions of quantification, multiplicity, and plenty. We begin with one place the wind can take Shakespeare's audiences – the shores of a deserted island. We begin, that is, with the shipwreck narrative of *The Tempest*.

The castaway plot offers a unique opportunity to think about what it means for an individual to exist in relation to others. After all, these stories often imagine heroes beginning society anew, formulating political relationships, and questioning the values of violence. Daniel Defoe's *Robinson Crusoe* (1719), for example, begins as a story of isolation, but it ultimately asks questions about what it means (and what it takes) to have a life in common with others. This is not to say that Crusoe crafts an ideal society; instead, he re-establishes the political and hierarchical structures that he learned in Europe. The native Friday becomes his slave and his island a small kingdom; it's hardly a utopia, and Crusoe's claim to love Friday as a friend does little to excuse the justifications for slavery.

These narratives of loss and survival, however, can also give glimpses of reconciliation and equality. Consider for a moment *The Martian* (Dir. Ridley Scott, 2015, based on the 2011 novel by Andy Weir), itself a loose adaptation of Defoe's novel that ponders questions about how to be with others.[5] This tale of survival on the planet-sized desert island of Mars asks us to think profoundly about peace on Earth. The stranded astronaut can be rescued only through cooperation as different countries must work together in order to solve problems and "bring him home," as the film's tagline demanded. The solution comes when the National Space Administration in China willingly shares a classified booster rocket with NASA in the United States. The collaboration at the heart of this tale recalls the origin for our English word "peace." The term derives from the Latin *pax*, which meant primarily "a pact" or mutual agreement between parties. In the quick turn of events that resolves the film's conflicts, a technology with military implications is used to save a single life rather than to take many, and more open collaboration and communication between rivals is established. The story does eventually serve the American character at the heart of *The Martian*, meaning that global resources end up supporting an American enterprise. For at least a moment, though, a global future seems possible, and one wonders what the space program for either nation will look like in the future. Sometimes (but not always) the shipwreck narrative, a story about being stranded and having to fight to stay alive, can imagine amicability and peaceful relations. Crusoe will stake out his colony, just as *The Martian*'s castaway does, but the questions linger: Could there be another arrangement?

Crusoe and Mark Watney, the astronaut of *The Martian*, can hardly be held up as icons of pacifism or understanding.

Instead, they look like the heroes of colonialism, both claiming ownership over distant lands. In that act of violence, however accidental, they share something else in common: They both love to count things. Crusoe keeps detailed records of his possessions, and the novel at points takes on the appearance of a ledger. He even goes so far as to count his debts toward God, listing a balance sheet of his religious deeds and sins. Watney never goes that far, but he similarly calculates the rations that will help him survive on Mars. If Bob Dylan asks these heroes "How many roads must a man walk down?," they would most likely have a number in mind. This meticulous bookkeeping helps them survive, but it also gets in the way of peace. To discover another relationship, they'll need to imagine a life unbound by quantification.

In the early modern period, island stories could produce alternative relationships. This is certainly true of Thomas More's *Utopia* (1516), in which a traveler encounters the ideal society on a remote island. Francis Bacon's *The New Atlantis* (1627) followed in that tradition, offering an image of the ideal scientific community. Not long after, Henry Neville's *The Isle of Pines* (1668) presented the story of castaways discovering an unknown society on a distant island. The impulse is there – to see how different people lived. The island makes that thought experiment possible; all it takes is a mysterious wind to push the reader there. Shakespeare found his direct inspiration for *The Tempest* in William Strachey's *A True Reportory of the Wracke and Redemption of Sir Thomas Gates, Knight* (1610), a re-telling of a very real shipwreck in the Bermudas. Scholars have long associated *The Tempest* with this book; both feature shipwrecks, makeshift societies, and the threat of rebellion. Both narratives, that is, ask how people get along, and whether we'll all end up at war with one another.

As Shakespeare's play opens, it is unclear just exactly what kind of story this will be. Will it be a comedy? A tragedy? A revenge tragedy? Of course, the narrative will resolve in reconciliation and forgiveness for some of the characters but not all of them. Like the castaway stories that will follow Shakespeare's, the play wonders about the limits of peace-making efforts. Bob Dylan ironically says the answer is blowing in the wind. *The Tempest* says much of the same; don't try counting to get the answer, because that approach gets the question of peace wrong.

THE WINDS OF WAR

The first scene of the play calls into question a frequent critique of peacemakers: Their tactics are made futile in the face of reality. Those who want to make peace through talking become pretty useless when nobody listens. Shakespeare opens with the ship in the middle of the storm, the chaos throwing into doubt the value of rational conversation. The Boatswain calls out to Gonzalo, "an honest old counsellor of Naples," and berates the nobleman for his obvious uselessness. A sailor knows his way in the storm, a courtier not so much:

> You are a councillor; if you can command these elements to silence and work the peace of the present, we will not hand a rope more. Use your authority. If you cannot, give thanks you have lived so long and make yourself ready in your cabin for the mischance of the hour, if it so hap. [To the Mariners] Cheerly, good hearts! [To Gonzalo] Out of our way, I say!
> (1.1.18–24)

At first, what the Boatswain says does seem to be self-evident. How could a "councillor" affect the weather? Surely this is not a situation when the sage Gonzalo can "work the peace" in a way that an advisor from the court might be known for. Yet the Boatswain's lines recall the exclamation he made just moments before: "What cares these roarers for the name of king?" (1.1.15–16). The irony of these earlier lines is that the "roarers" (waves) in fact do follow the command of a ruler. They are the doing of Prospero, who had been "the Duke of Milan, and/A prince of power" (1.2.53–54). Having been something like a king in his life, Prospero is now, by all accounts, the king of the island. The roarers *do care about* what a king thinks. Moreover, the king who controls these particular waves used to be counseled by Gonzalo. It is not outside the realm of possibility that Gonzalo, honest counselor that he is, could "work the peace of the present" if Prospero were in earshot. Gonzalo might not literally direct the wind; his work involves more subtle forms of influence through informed advice. Far from futile, the advice to "work the peace" could actually do something this time.

In Shakespeare's time, many would agree with the logic that the ruler determined whether a nation should be primarily war- or peace- seeking. Treatises both on the nation and on the household described the king as God's appointed ruler on Earth. In turn, male subjects were kings of their own households, and their wives and children were understood as their subjects. The kingdom was a large household comprising many tiny households. We hear echoes of this hierarchy in Erasmus' description of the peaceful nation:

> [Princes'] intention towards their country should be that of a father towards his family. A king should think himself great if the subjects he rules are of the very best, happy if he makes his people happy, exalted if the men he governs enjoy the

> greatest measure of freedom, wealthy if they are wealthy,
> prosperous if his cities prosper in unbroken peace.[6]

Here, in "The Complaint of Peace," Erasmus articulates the possibilities for pacifism when its members bond through the bloodlines of family and through their shared emotions. Erasmus shows us that *Henry V*'s notion of soldiers as a "band of brothers" can be re-imagined as a model for pacifism. The king cannot be happy unless his family of subjects are happy, and they aren't happy unless at peace. When we read of the "great" subjects as well as the "prosperous" community, we can't help but think of the idea that we heard several early modern writers assert in the previous chapter: Periods of peace are deeply connected to economic plenty. Erasmus goes on:

> And the nobles and holders of office should model their
> attitude on that of their prince, judging everything by the
> country's interests; by this means they will also have acted
> properly in their own interests.[7]

So the subordinate leaders will imitate the king, who takes cues from the public. Even the pursuit of personal "interests" ends up serving the ends of a pacifist state. Shakespeare will reinforce such logic, emphasizing that peace-making can be a top-down affair. *The Tempest* will resolve with the characters gathered together under the power of Prospero, who will spur peace and reconciliation among his former subjects. Their peace is his peace. But as we work toward that conclusion, let's not forget this ruler's old counselor Gonzalo.

In another key text of Shakespeare's day, the Italian author Baldesar Castiglione offers his advice to those who attend a prince and make their living at court. This work, *The Book of the Courtier* (1528), served as a self-help manual for those looking to increase their influence around the monarchy. In the final sections, Castiglione implies that a counselor shouldn't just help a ruler enforce violence and domination; instead, a true courtier will help a ruler find peace. In this, Castiglione opposes Machiavelli, the "realist" advisor to early modern kings. Castiglione finds company here with Erasmus.[8] His character Ottaviano says, "it is also the office of the good prince to establish his people in law and ordinances that they may live in ease and peace, without danger and with dignity, and may worthily enjoy this end of their actions, namely tranquility."[9] The courtier guides the prince to true value – in this case, that value is peace. The ruler must learn that "to be always at war, without seeking to achieve the end which is peace, is not right."[10] A worthwhile counselor should help that lesson along. In that, Gonzalo does his duty.

After the shipwreck, the stranded men meander around the island with no way of knowing that they are working toward a confrontation with Prospero, the Duke they had once conspired against. These former villains inevitably generate new forms of tension. Noblemen conspire to murder each other. Servants plot to take over the island. One of the castaways, Ferdinand, falls in love with Prospero's daughter Miranda. These characters operate from a place of lack because they desire higher status or more money. By separating the castaways into different groups, Shakespeare showcases different forms of discord that can drive the friction from which war emerges. The exception seems to be Ferdinand, who wanders alone until he meets Miranda and realizes that he would rather make love than war. Even he starts from a place of lack, as he is a prince without a princess.

To discover peace, he will ironically have to learn "plenty" first. He'll have to learn that abundance doesn't follow from peace, but that conceiving of abundance just might lead these groups to peace.

At one point, Prospero's spirit-servant Ariel takes the form of a harpy and attacks one group of castaways, crying out:

> But remember,
> For that's my business to you, that you three
> From Milan did supplant good Prospero;
> Exposed unto the sea, which hath requit it,
> Him and his innocent child; for which foul deed,
> The powers, delaying, not forgetting, have
> Incensed the seas and shores, yea, all the creatures,
> Against your peace.
>
> (3.3.68–74)

Ariel suggests that the natural order is disturbed when evil men plot against a good one. The sea will "requite" – as in repay – these villains. They have incurred a debt that demands repayment, meaning that Ariel operates in the language of scarcity and counting. The language of plenty awaits. In the same scene Ariel informs the traitors that they cannot withstand him or the force of his master's revenge plot because "the elements/Of whom your swords are tempered may as well/Wound the loud winds" (3.3.61–63). Susan Harlan suggests that Ariel's use of "tempered" points to the men's lack of temperance or virtue.[11] The storm is thus both a superior force of justice in the present and a consequence arising from their past crimes. It appears as if the tempest was both part of Prospero's revenge plot and an expression of the natural world being "incensed." This term was newly coined in

English during Shakespeare's time to mean angry (as it does today) and was derived from the Latin word "*incendere,*" to set on fire. Recognizing the origins of the word, we can hear how powerfully upset the world has become at the usurpation of Prospero. The ocean is on fire with rage, and it wants its repayment.

Gonzalo, though, can see a way through the scorekeeping and violent retribution – by imagining infinite goods, and so infinite forgiveness.

UTOPIA IN IDLENESS

The same ocean, but another time and another disposition. Upon his exile, Prospero was set adrift in a small boat with Miranda. The sea carried them gently to this island, and the things they carried were just necessary supplies (including Prospero's books) given to them by the old counselor Gonzalo. Prospero describes how, "by providence divine,"

> Some food we had, and some fresh water, that
> A noble Neapolitan, Gonzalo,
> Out of his charity – who being then appointed
> Master of this design – did give us; with
> Rich garments, linens, stuffs, and necessaries
> Which since have steaded much. So, of his gentleness,
> Knowing I loved my books, he furnished me
> From mine own library with volumes that
> I prize above my dukedom.
>
> (1.2.160–168)

Though they arrive with these few items given by this counselor marked by "charity" and "gentleness," Prospero and Miranda live in a state of lack in their island home. They have little in terms of companionship and dwell in a "poor cell" (1.2.20). *The Tempest* ultimately will offer us little in terms of a reunion between Gonzalo and Prospero. During their separation, Prospero was ordering his island – with Ariel and Caliban in forced servitude – and plotting his revenge. Hardly charitable, Prospero instead seeks repayment. But Gonzalo seems to have been doing his own thinking about what went wrong in Milan. The same "charity" he showed the exiled Duke will help to imagine the play's final moments of forgiveness and peace.

When one of his fellow castaways asks about his vision for a society on their newfound island home, Gonzalo describes an ideal commonwealth as one with "all men idle." Shakespeare gets the passage from a contemporary writer, Michel Montaigne. In his essay "Of Cannibals" (c. 1580), Montaigne writes of the native populations in the New World, imagining them living in an ideal state. Shakespeare follows this essay as Gonzalo muses,

> I'th' commonwealth I would by contraries
> Execute all things. For no kind of traffic
> Would I admit, no name of magistrate;
> Letters should not be known; riches, poverty,
> And use of service, none; contract, succession,
> Bourn, bound of land, tilth, vineyard, none;
> No use of metal, corn, or wine, or oil;
> No occupation; all men idle, all;
> And women too – but innocent and pure;
> No sovereignty.
>
> (2.1.147–156)

The vision not only longs for a simpler age that has passed but also desires to remake the world going forward. The lack of writing, class distinctions, and technology sounds like a simpler world that one might fantasize had existed at the dawn of humanity. But Gonzalo is talking about a world that he thinks is still possible. From one angle, this place that meets everyone's needs resembles a type of post-scarcity economy envisioned by science fiction authors today. As we'll see in the next chapter, speculative fiction pursues that same impulse in imagining utopia. From another angle, Gonzalo's world sounds like the one posited in John Lennon's 1971 hit "Imagine." The song urges us to picture a world without hunger, greed, or religion. The result would be "nothing to kill or die for." We would find "all people living in peace," and consequently "the world will be as one."[12] Gonzalo's speech and Lennon's song spell out the logic by which plenty brings peace. When there is enough of things that everyone wants, we end up without the things we don't want, including violence. Gonzalo is capable of such imagination, and such speculation will help Prospero to forgive. He, like the audience, must come to understand that even if physical goods are limited, emotional relationships aren't.

When Antonio (Prospero's younger brother and usurper) dismisses Gonzalo's vision as nonsensical, the counselor continues,

> All things in common nature should produce
> Without sweat or endeavor. Treason, felony,
> Sword, pike, knife, gun, or need of any engine,
> Would I not have; but nature should bring forth
> Of it own kind all foison, all abundance,
> To feed my innocent people.
>
> (2.1.159–164)[13]

This society has neither crime nor weapons, meaning there's little to no violence here. It is "all abundance" and its people "innocent." One might say that Gonzalo's a dreamer, but this is not the only text where we find a vision of a peaceful group, loving in idleness. This group takes us back to the forest court in *As You Like It*, the country estate in *Much Ado About Nothing*, and the noblemen's retreat in *Love's Labour's Lost*. Gonzalo's commonwealth exists only in his mind at this point, but as Erasmus described earlier, the peaceful nation stems from the pacifist disposition of its rule. The aging counselor promises that "I would with such perfection govern, sir,/T'excel the Golden Age" (2.1.167–168). His vision does indeed sound like that ideal age the ancients called the "Golden Age." Ovid's *Metamorphoses*, for example, describes the world of long ago this way:

> Men knew none other countries yet, than where themselves did keep:
> There was no town enclosed yet, with walls and ditches deep.
> No horn nor trumpet was in use, no sword nor helmet worn,
> The world was such, that soldiers' help might easily be forborne.[14]

This idealized world, a world that some early moderns believed might return in their lifetimes, is a world with plenty to be shared and subsequently without war or military. Nobody has divided it into pieces, claiming some of the world for their own and denying it to others. All was one. For Gonzalo, this "myth functioning as a memory," as Raymond Williams described the Golden Age, constitutes a vision of a future even better than a mythical past.[15] Gonzalo, then, participates in a sort of anachronism, seeing in the past a possible future. In that move, he again looks like a sci-fi writer, or the "unhistorical" history we discussed in our introduction – the historian who finds hope in anachronism.

Peace, in other words, will follow from the imaginative indulgence that occurs after the shipwreck. For the briefest of moments, this speech suggests a new world that could be established on the island or, better yet, that the characters from the island will come back to civilization with notions about a new way of living in peace and in common. Like the vision of peace and freedom articulated by Bob Dylan's non-protesting protest anthem from which the chapter takes its title, Gonzalo's proposal is straightforward and reliant on the very simplicity of its formulation. Gonzalo's vision suggests that the key to everlasting peace is right in front of them. It is the island that they have been blown to, the one that ultimately frustrates repayment or revenge. The wind can't answer Dylan's questions of "how many?"; it also refuses that answer here on Prospero's island.

But the play ends neither with the castaways staying on the island nor with an unquestioned commitment to make the counselor's imagined world a reality. It ends in a place of ambiguity, of the sort that Dylan might approve.

PROSPERO'S PARDONING

Although the end of *The Tempest* does promise the end of immediate conflict, it does not particularly promise a better world on the horizon. Prospero brings the island world into order during the final act of the play. His former usurpers will relinquish control in order for the noble Ferdinand to rule with Miranda by his side. Caliban and servant-castaways fail in their own plot to take control of the island. And Prospero's own pledge to break his staff and drown his book suggests not only a laying down of weapons but also a moment of *forgive and forget*. Judith Pollmann suggests, "from the Middle Ages until the nineteenth century, acts of oblivion were a favorite instrument in any peacemaker's toolkit."[16] Forgetting the past does seem to offer a way for this group to move forward, but it remains unclear whether this strategy makes way for avoiding violent impulses in the future. When Prospero confronts the men who betrayed him, he does so attired as the Duke of Milan. It makes one wonder whether his peace-making efforts can break the cycle of war and peace or whether they simply prop up a new hierarchy. Prospero proclaims, "I'll deliver all,/ And promise you calm seas, auspicious gales" (5.1.317–318). The sea will once more be calm as rightful order is restored in Milan. The "auspicious" gales hope for good fortune and perhaps place us in the status of "if" – that suspended tension of ongoing negotiation about what-might-be that can make peace possible.

In fact, as the play winds to its conclusions, we see that literal "if" appear over and over again. It moves Prospero to forgiveness by giving him the ability to hold multiple – sometimes contradictory – states of mind. From that plenty, one hopes that peace follows. Ariel explains to Prospero that the magician's charms have worked: The former conspirators against Prospero have been trapped and driven to the edge of despair. Ariel pleads, "Your charm so strongly works 'em/ That if you now beheld them your affections/Would become tender" (5.1.17–19). If you could just see the state of your enemies, you would become more merciful. That construction gives Prospero the ability to speculate. He can remain angry, but simultaneously he can imagine his opponents in ways that soften his anger. The "if" works its own kind of magic by revealing multiple possibilities. As the castaways awake and recognize Prospero, they also turn to "if" and try to work out what's real and what's not. This is the thinking that can lead toward peace. The King of Naples, for example, wonders whether Prospero truly appears on the island. He says, "if this be at all – a most strange story" (5.1.119), meaning, "If this is truly happening, it's a very strange story." The charms have confused the king, and he wonders what counts as truth. For all of the fear and anxiety Prospero has caused, he has also allowed other characters to consider alternatives to what they assume is true. "Realpolitik" and "hard truths" don't have much place here. Gonzalo agrees with the sentiment: "Whether this be/Or be not, I'll not swear" (5.1.123–124). In that state of mind, Prospero is both exiled and returned, just as criminals are both guilty and forgiven, just as the wronged can be both angry and forgiving. It is "strange" – a term that in Shakespeare's day means "exceptionally great" or "difficult to take in or account for."[17] Too much makes the whole ending "strange," and so it makes peace possible.

In another key moment, the king Alonso grieves the loss of his son, Ferdinand. In this case, Alonso is mistaken; he thinks Ferdinand was lost in the shipwreck, but Prospero once again plays tricks on his island visitors. Alonso says, "Irreparable is the loss, and patience/Says it is past her cure" (5.1.142–143). Repayment cannot suffice, at least in Alonso's mind. No surplus of goods or money can replace the lost son. When Prospero makes the grand revelation – showing Ferdinand playing chess with his love, Miranda – audiences may rightfully feel that the magician acts cruelly.

In a sense, Prospero has held this son hostage until the dukedom is restored. Upon seeing his living son, Alonso delivers yet another skeptical "if": "If this prove/A vision of the island, one dear son/Shall I lose twice" (5.1.178–180). This expression again creates multitudes, for Ferdinand momentarily survives and does not survive. The grief turns to peace once Alonso grasps the notion that loss can in fact be repaired. Even when one assumes the lack, Shakespeare spins things to surplus. Even the small cell and deserted island of Prospero become places of plenty. Miranda's most famous lines sum up the effect well: "O wonder! How many goodly creatures are there here!" (5.1.184–185). Folks keep showing up in the place she had assumed was deserted. In that plenty, the play moves to forgiveness. Prospero will return to his dukedom, past crimes fade, and hope returns. Miranda precedes Bob Dylan in uttering "how many?" – how many goodly creatures are there? The answer, of course, is blowing in the wind, to a pacifist future that is made peaceful by its ambiguity and multiple meanings.

As the play winds down, Prospero frees his "airy spirit" Ariel, finally fulfilling a long-standing promise. What about Caliban? The slave occupies a troubled place; he figures the imperialist violence of Robinson Crusoe and seemingly justifies Prospero's control of the island. The magus sends Caliban back to his cell, where forgiveness for conspiracy may await. It's a frustrating resolution, but one that leaves open the possibility for Caliban's freedom. Indeed, that's just how Julie Taymor stages the scene in her 2010 film; Caliban ascends a staircase and leaves the stage through a door that signifies his freedom (Figure 4.1).

He never looks back. So how many ways can *The Tempest* end?

Figure 4.1 Caliban being set free (*The Tempest*, Dir. Taymor, Touchstone Pictures, 2010)

The Tempest is listed as a "comedy" in the earliest collections of Shakespeare's works. And, like other comedies we've encountered in this book, it uses its epilogue to suggest a porous boundary between the experiences of the characters on stage and the emotions of the members of the audience. Alone on stage, Prospero says,

> Now my charms are all o'erthrown,
> And what strength I have's mine own,
> Which is most faint. Now 'tis true
> I must be here confined by you
> Or sent to Naples.
>
> (E.1–5)

When Prospero says his charms are "o'erthrown," he refers to giving up his magic. But the word reminds us that his dukedom was once overthrown, and now he has overthrown his usurper. This has still been a play about political force. Unlike Mars in *Venus and Adonis*, Prospero has not totally given up forceful solutions for more subtle forms of influence. He goes on to emphasize that he has dispelled his weapons and now relies on others:

> Now I want
> Spirits to enforce, art to enchant;
> And my ending is despair
> Unless I be relieved by prayer,
> Which pierces so, that it assaults
> Mercy itself, and frees all faults.
> As you from crimes would pardoned be,
> Let your indulgence set me free.
>
> (E.13–20)

It is a speech about peace, but it is filled with the language of war. He admits to his "crimes" and seeks "pardon" to be released from "confines" and hopes against "assaults" on mercy.[18] In fact, he frames his request for pardon in terms of the audience needing forgiveness, too. His off-hand phrase, "as you from crimes would pardoned be," suggests that both he and the audience can feel a bit less guilty about past indiscretions by way of applause. In a play that Sarah Beckwith describes as "an exploration of the work of theater in the work of penitence," this shipwreck narrative has turned out to enable a working through of issues for its characters and audience.[19] Everyone is granted "indulgence," a term carrying the notion of "over-lenient treatment" as well as the religious sense of "remission of the punishment which is still due to sin after sacramental absolution."[20] Debts are forgiven through the excess of emotion.

It is all well and good, but one might hear echoes of Pandarus' suggestion that the audience are bawds like him at the end of *Troilus and Cressida*. The play affirms forgiveness, reconciliation, and justice. We just can't forget that this places us back in the cycle of inevitable violence, and that we'll need the magical charms of "if" at some other point. The good news is that there's always plenty of "if" to go around.

SHAKESPEARE'S LAST WORDS ON PEACE: *CYMBELINE*

In the next chapter, we'll come back to *The Tempest* as a narrative of the future in science fictional adaptations of Shakespeare's work. Before we do that, though, let us touch briefly upon another of Shakespeare's late plays that links forgiveness to peace. With its dozens of revelations and bewildering number of plots, *Cymbeline* is often understood as a combination of Shakespearean tropes and theatrical genres. As Brian Gibbons puts it, "Surveying the play from a distance we can see that Shakespeare has ransacked theatre high and low, recent and ancient to present a whole variety of styles and genres through which a history can be told, (and this constitutes a small history of theatre in itself)."[21] This is a strange play, and by that, we mean it indulges excess in almost every way, nicking plot points from *The Rape of Lucrece*, *As You Like It*, *Othello*, *Romeo and Juliet*, and so many others. For those reasons alone, *Cymbeline* draws together many of the pacifist concepts we have seen thus far.

Cymbeline takes place in the ancient era of peace known as the *Pax Romana*. Broadly speaking, the play dramatizes the conflicts between ancient Rome and Britain as they engage in the final battles that predate a long period of peace. At issue is the requirement that the British pay tribute to Rome, a penalty that the British King Cymbeline resists. That political plot persists alongside another comedic plot that follows King Cymbeline's daughter Innogen as she attempts to reunite with her beloved husband Poshumus. When experiencing a moment of particular despair, Innogen announces, "Plenty and peace breeds cowards, hardness ever/Of hardiness is mother" (3.6.21–22). We have heard this logic before. The idea that periods without war are characterized by an abundance of resources was prominent in *A Midsummer Night's Dream* and in Gonzalo's vision of the ideal commonwealth in *The Tempest*. Here, though, Innogen follows *Coriolanus* and suggests that the periods of plenty make people weak. Having enough means not needing to be brave and not being prepared for war. Such a philosophy did undergird the *Pax Romana*, which was a peace that comes about after the Romans have conquered their rivals through force and through war. Given that "any discussion of Roman Peace – whatever this truly meant – should be set in the context of Roman conquest," we should read Innogen's declaration with a somewhat suspicious eye.[22] The period of peace between Britain and Rome was perhaps only war by another means. The ancient historian Tacitus wrote of Roman imperialism in Britain: "they create desolation and call it peace."[23] Innogen's concern that peace breeds weakness (a claim that the play does not necessarily bear out) echoes an idea voiced by Francis Bacon, who writes that "a just and honorable war is the true exercise [because] war is like the heat of exercise and serves to keep the body in health. For in a slothful peace, both courage will effeminate and manners corrupt."[24] It should be noted that Innogen posits this logic when things seem at their worst as she has wandered into the wilderness in a time of war and seeks shelter in a cave. However, the tides will change quickly, suggesting that her outlook seemed very much informed by her need to convince herself that she was capable of survival. *Cymbeline*, of course, delights in busyness, and any claim that peace is boring or enervating is offset by the myriad twists that come to characterize this peace.

Later in the play, the male hero Posthumus will be visited in a dream by his deceased ancestors, accompanied by the Roman god Jupiter. This divinity leaves behind a tablet that gives a cryptic prophecy begging for interpretation. It doesn't give clear answers, but it does imagine a time of peace that will come for Britain:

> Whenas a lion's whelp shall, to himself unknown, without seeking find, and be embraced by a piece of tender air; and when from a stately cedar shall be lopped branches which, being dead many years, shall after revive, be jointed to the old stock, and freshly grow; then shall Posthumus end his miseries, Britain be fortunate and flourish in peace and plenty.
>
> (5.5.232–238)

If Innogen earlier dismissed the links between plenty and peace, this prophecy offers another take. It repeats "peace and plenty" but does not present that connection as a negative. When we look closely at the inscription, we notice that "peace and plenty" have a parallel relationship with "fortunate and flourish." Rather than a stupor that Innogen fears, peaceful times are desired, wished for, and linked with progress. Posthumus reacts to the tablet this way:

> 'Tis still a dream, or else such stuff as madmen
> Tongue and brain not; either both or nothing,
> Or senseless speaking, or a speaking such
> As sense cannot untie. Be what it is,
> The action of my life is like it, which I'll keep,
> If but for sympathy.
>
> (5.5.238–243)

It is interesting that Posthumus considers the visitation and perhaps the words on the tablet to be "a dream." The term recalls Puck's apology at the end of *A Midsummer Night's Dream*. In this case, though, the dream here carries forward into the waking world, when the words are read aloud in the court. The prophecy in turn informs not only the states of Rome and Britain but also the audience in the early modern theater. We should note that Posthumus cannot make sense of what he reads. The tablet looks like "senseless speaking," much like a song that doesn't give the answers it seems to promise. Not that Posthumus will give up – he keeps the tablet "if but for the" resemblance to his own life. He willingly entertains the ambiguity in his own experience and so pushes the play forward to "peace and plenty."

During the incredibly busy last scene, the political plots and the romantic plots come together. The lovers reunite just as King Cymbeline prepares to affirm British allegiance to the Roman Empire and its *Pax Romana*. Cymbeline is also reunited with his two missing sons – children whom he had presumed dead. Like Alonso, Cymbeline learns that loss is impermanent, that absence turns suddenly to surplus. In this play, even the dead can rise; Posthumus' name tells us just that. Innogen, upon learning that she has two brothers, remarks, "I have got two worlds by't" (5.6.375). She comes to embrace the excess. The court's Soothsayer then returns to the tablet left by Jupiter and explains its meanings:

> The lofty cedar, royal Cymbeline,
> Personates thee, and thy lopped branches point
> Thy two sons forth, who, by Belarius stol'n,
> For many years thought dead, are now revived,
> To the majestic cedar joined, whose issue
> Promises Britain peace and plenty
>
> (5.6.453–458)

The announcement not only signals restitution in the closing of the play but also underscores that Innogen's fears about peace and plenty were unfounded. The word "joined" emphasizes that this is about creating a new wholeness, a form of mending. It would go too far to say that this is the same "cedar" that Prospero splits with his power. However, it is not too much to note here that Prospero's power (a power that he relinquishes in favor of peaceful resolution) splits trees and that Cymbeline's power (a power that builds alliances) joins great trees. The cedar here is the family line, the genealogical branches of the family tree, and it is the chain of linkages that connects seed to outcome. More and more come together in Shakespeare's final visions of pacifism. The prophecy of peace leads Cymbeline to announce immediately, "My peace we will begin" (5.6.459).

The Soothsayer's use of the phrase "promises Britain peace and plenty" does remind us that the auspicious vision of the future is speculative. It imagines a Britain of the ancient period, far before Shakespeare's own audience was alive. The play, that is, deals with anachronism in its claims of peace – this period has already passed but is described as if it were to come. And, although the play's audience may know that the hoped-for peace doesn't take hold permanently, it does suggest that such hopes are renewable. The speculative might-have-been could incentivize playgoers to consider what the future still might be. The Soothsayer adds, "The fingers of the powers above do tune/The harmony of this peace" (5.6.466–467). The lines suggest that the gods desire peaceful relations and also suggest that peace results from a type of concord. Indeed, "harmony" points to the musicality of regularized iambic pentameter in Shakespeare's plays. Works of literature, in the harmony of their lines that are performed and published, might have a role in encouraging pacifism.[25]

In the final lines of the play, Cymbeline declares,

> Publish we this peace
> To all our subjects. Set we forward, let
> A Roman and a British ensign wave
> Friendly together. So through Lud's town march,
> And in the temple of great Jupiter
> Our peace we'll ratify, seal it with feasts.
> Set on there. Never was a war did cease,
> Ere bloody hands were washed, with such a peace.
> (5.6.478–485)

The last word of one of Shakespeare's last plays is "peace." Intriguingly, the word "publish" suggested several meanings in the early modern period. It meant "to make public or generally known" and "to make generally accessible or available for acceptance or use (a work of art, information, etc.)."[26] So, the actors make public this model of peaceful accord between people and nations, just as the play's appearance in Shakespeare's collected works publishes an account of this peace for posterity. In other words, the text itself spreads peace, perhaps just by virtue of its multiple plots, multiple choices, and multiple ambiguities.

Shakespeare knew what he was doing even in 1609–1610, when his troupe first performed *Cymbeline*. James VI of Scotland had just been named James I, King of England, in 1603. His accession represented a newfound union between Scotland and England, a promising sign that the real violence between the people of the British Isles might come to resolution. James also sought to end another ongoing conflict – the intermittent wars with Spain, both in the exploration of the New World and in the religious conflicts that permeated the early modern period. James I arrived as a peacemaker, bound to end the wars. This king, who according to one legend "could not stand the sight of an unsheathed sword," modeled himself as the *Rex Pacificus*, ready to usher in a new era just as Shakespeare was winding down his theatrical career.[27] In a book titled *The Wonderfull Yeare* (1603), the author Thomas Dekker celebrated James in language strikingly similar to that of *Cymbeline* and *The Tempest* alike:

> The Cedar of [Elizabeth's] government which stood alone and bare no fruit, is changed now to an Olive, upon whose spreading branches grow both Kings and Queenes. Oh it were able to fill a hundred pair of writing tables with notes, but to see the parts plaid in the compass of one hour on the stage of this newfound world![28]

The branches grow again, and with them comes the peaceful "newfound world" – one thinks of Prospero's island. Treaties followed James, and although his reign did deal with its share of conspiracies and conflicts, the ambition was there. This was the peaceful king, ready to make treaties with former foes.

That's not to say that all of James' subjects were happy with the new directions in English politics. A number of protests appeared, wary that a peaceful age would weaken the nation and leave it vulnerable. Among the disgruntled were names such as Francis Bacon and Sir Walter Raleigh. This echoed other writers such as Thomas Wilson, who in 1600 insisted that "the long continuance of peace ha[s] bred a inward canker and unrest in men's minds, the people doing nothing but jar and wrangle with one another."[29] On the other hand, some poets embraced the possibilities of peace-making. John Stradling composed *Beati Pacifici* – "Blessed Are the Peacemakers" – in 1623, addressing it to King James I. Stradling writes,

> Sweet is the name of Peace, but sweeter farre
> The thing itself, experience proves it true:
> An Adage old doth tell me, Sweet is War.
> To whom? To him that War yet never knew.
> If any list to try before he trust,
> Such will approve my saying true and just.[30]

The sentiment supports James. Stradling embraces peace as God's will, and true virtue over and above anything that war can offer. Shakespeare wrote *Cymbeline* and *The Tempest* decades earlier, but the sentiment was already there.

In the beginning of his poem Stradling has this to say: "Peace may be understood more ways than one,/The world is full of ambiguity."[31] This chapter began with ambiguity, so it's fitting to end there. In its variety of plots, *Cymbeline* does suggest that things could turn out any number of ways, so many that one shouldn't even bother counting. But from that multiplicity emerges peaceful thinking. If things could end in a *Pax Romana*, then James I can know that his era of peace too is possible. How many histories can the text allow? Enough to allow forgiveness and indulge the dreamers who refuse the "inevitability" of war. Or rather, the answer is blowing in the wind.

Let's then move to today's dreamers, those who also want to write alternative histories. We speak of the science fiction writers looking for utopia in the present era.

NOTES

1 Quoted in Clinton Heylin, *Revolution in the Air: The Songs of Bob Dylan, 1957–1973* (Chicago: Chicago Review Press, 2009), 78.

2 Quoted in Michael Gray, *The Bob Dylan Encyclopedia* (London and New York: Continuum International, 2006), 64.

3 Bob Dylan, "Blowin' in the Wind," recorded 1963, track 1 on The Freewheelin' Bob Dylan, Sony Music, digital album.

4 Quoted in Gray, *The Bob Dylan Encyclopedia*, 64.
5 For more on *The Martian*, see Kyle Pivetti, "The king of mars: The Martian's scientific empire and Robinson Crusoe," in *The Cinematic Eighteenth Century: History, Culture, and Adaptation*, ed. Srividhya Swaminathan and Steven W. Thomas (Abingdon and New York: Routledge, 2017), 118–38.
6 Desiderius Erasmus, "A complaint of peace spurned and rejected by the whole world," in *Collected Works of Erasmus: Literary and Educational Writings*, vol. 27, ed. A. H. T. Levi, trans. Betty Radice (Toronto: University of Toronto Press, 1986), 289–322, 311.
7 Ibid., 311.
8 See Stephen Kolsky, "Peace and War in Castiglione's Courtier," *Explorations in Renaissance Culture* 37.2 (2011): 17–38, 25.
9 Baldesar Castiglione, *The Book of the Courtier*, ed. Daniel Javitch (New York: W. W. Norton & Co., 2002), 225.
10 Ibid., 225.
11 Susan Harlan, *Memories of War in Early Modern England: Armor and Militant Nostalgia in Marlowe, Sidney, and Shakespeare* (New York: Palgrave Macmillan, 2016), 259.
12 John Lennon, "Imagine" (Apple Records, 1971).
13 The vision closely resembles Montaigne's description of a seemingly primitive society in his essay "On Cannibals" but with some crucial differences. Montaigne describes a people he knows of who live without commerce, political superiority, riches, poverty, contracts, property ownership, hard work, greed, and so on. Yet this group does engage in violent, physical conflict. They go to war and eventually eat their prisoners. Gonzalo imagines a different possibility for his simple society.
14 All English quotations from the *Metamorphoses* are drawn from Ovid, *Metamorphoses*, trans. Arthur Golding (London: W. Series, 1567), which is available through the Perseus Project. This quotation appears in Book 1, lines 97–100.
15 Raymond Williams, *The Country and the City* (Oxford: Oxford University Press, 1975), 43.
16 Judith Pollmann, *Memory in Early Modern Europe* (Oxford: Oxford University Press, 2017), 141.
17 "Strange, adj.," OED Online, January 2018, Oxford University Press, www.oed.com, accessed March 17, 2018.
18 We might understand this scene as confessional, as Prospero admits to having committed crimes and asks for forgiveness. John Bossy suggests

that the rite of confession was "lost in the peace-making process" after the Reformation in England. John Bossy, *Peace in the Post-Reformation* (Cambridge: Cambridge University Press, 1998), 78.

19 Sarah Beckwith, *Shakespeare and the Grammar of Forgiveness* (Ithaca: Cornell University Press, 2012), 153.
20 "Indulgence, n.," OED Online, January 2018, Oxford University Press, www.oed.com, accessed March 17, 2018.
21 Brian Gibbons, *Shakespeare and Multiplicity* (Cambridge: Cambridge University Press, 1993), 24.
22 Adrian Goldsworthy, *Pax Romana: War, Peace, and Conquest in the Roman World* (New Haven: Yale University Press, 2017), 18.
23 For a discussion of Roman rule throughout the empire as maintained by forced peace, see Mary Beard, *SPQR: A History of Ancient Rome* (New York: W. W. Norton & Co., 2016), 475–522.
24 Francis Bacon, *Francis Bacon: The Major Works*, ed. Brian Vickers (Oxford: Oxford University Press, 2008), 402.
25 For more on plays and other forms of literature as the forums for discussing the possibilities of peace, see Alexandra Gajda, "Debating War and Peace in Late Elizabethan England," *The Historical Journal* 52.4 (2009): 851–78.
26 "Publish, v.," OED Online, January 2018, Oxford University Press, www.oed.com, accessed March 17, 2018.
27 James Doelman, *King James I and the Religious Culture of England* (Cambridge: DS Brewer, 2000), 86.
28 Quoted in Doelman, *King James I and the Religious Culture of England*, 87.
29 Quoted in Lawrence Stone, *Social Change and Revolution in England 1540–1640* (New York: Barnes & Noble, 1965), 119.
30 John Stradling, *Beati Pacifici* (London: Felix Kingston, 1623), 3.
31 Ibid., 1.

Another world was possible

Five

In its first sentences, Harry Harrison's short story "Fragment of a Manuscript" does not feel like science fiction. The piece is featured in *Microcosmic Tales*, a volume of short-short stories co-edited by the legendary Isaac Asimov in 1980, but Harrison begins with the dry and detached tone of a scholar sitting in one of the oldest landmarks of academia: "I found the two fragments of parchment, tied together with a bit of leather cord, behind one of the older bookcases in the Bodleian Library in Oxford."[1] Our narrator discovers the manuscript by pure chance. When he chases a lost coin behind a bookcase, the researcher finds pages long hidden from other curious readers. He reacts with proper — that is to say, boring — discretion. "In all truth I can lay no claims as to their authenticity, as to the authenticity of the writer that is, though their undoubted great age has been verified by certain chemical tests."[2] With further reference to texts of the 16th century, including *Orlando Furioso* and *The Faerie Queene*, the narrator dates the fragment to the 1590s. If he were correct, the find would be monumental: lost fragments of parchment that reveal Shakespeare's original plans for *A Midsummer Night's Dream*. And here Harrison's story takes its turn to science fiction.

The manuscript reimagines Act 3 Scene 1, when the rude mechanicals work out the "comedy of Pyramus and Thisbe" (3.1.8–9). In this draft, though, Bottom and the others collaborate on a futuristic play of rockets and aliens called the "comedy of Lunar Man." What we can gather of the plot centers around a moon man who arrives on Earth ready to deliver his Renaissance equivalent of "Take me to your leader." The mechanicals bicker about the special effects and performance, echoing many of the same bits from the actual *Midsummer*. Bottom, for instance, worries about staging Pyramus' suicide in the original play, but in Harrison's story, he frets about rockets: "First, landeth here a spatial ship, with roar and bluster; which the ladies cannot abide."[3] The solution? Bottom says, "The thought of rockets we must disabuse, we for a stellar barque a null-G ship will use."[4] The language only gets more surprisingly technical as they discuss the landing, the Lunar Man's entrance, and his first words. Bottom explains that the speech "we did copy from the book, chained there in church. How Lunar man sailed safe the sea of space, with cunning coils did achieve null-G and, with parlous speed, escape velocity."[5] Harrison gets the rhythms of Shakespeare's dialogue – the alliterative repetitions in "sailed safe the sea of space" – while adding the curious language of modern-day space travel. He also includes a dig at the church, which presumably houses secret knowledge of anti-gravity but protects its anti-science agenda by keeping it chained up. This Shakespeare is even more prescient and rebellious than we would have imagined; in science fiction, he foresees a future that breaks the chains of religious constraint.

Harrison ends his story with a winking line. After two pages of Bottom's sci-fi riddled dialogue, we get this: "A scrawled note across the last lines of the manuscript reads: *No, will not do, the market still unripe for SF. Rewrite – fantasy still best. Must buy book of fairy tales.*"[6] So Shakespeare apparently went on to write the familiar *Midsummer*, replacing his null-G ships with the fairies and magic we know. For a brief instance, though, Shakespeare was allowed to speculate on the future and its technical possibilities. It's an appealing fantasy in its own right – a towering literary genius who anachronistically becomes the purveyor of a genre he could not have known in the 1590s.

Harrison is not alone in drawing Shakespeare into the world of science fiction. The Renaissance writer shows up frequently in the speculative genres, asking questions about the nature of humanity, the value of literature, and the costs of war. He participates in the political questions that linger beneath the spaceships and wormholes. As Peter Paik puts it, science fiction is a "vital instrument for the investigation of the contingencies governing political life, the forces that structure and dissolve collective existence, by providing the readers in which familiar realities are destabilized and transformed."[7] Bringing Shakespeare into that mix introduces a curious paradox of the type that we see in Harrison's "Fragment of a Manuscript": a writer from our past who helps us to imagine alternatives for our future. In that, we will argue, speculative Shakespeare can serve as a means to pacifism. His plays become the conduit through which the sci-fi writer can envision another possible world defined by peace, both in the future and in the past. His visions just might give us alternatives for seeing how humanity got here and where it could go.

We take the phrase "possible world" from the World Social Forum, an annual meeting of groups who protest neoliberalism, globalization, and capitalist interests. In its own terms, the World Social Forum is "the representation of a new democratic cosmopolitanism, a new anti-capitalist transnationalism" that experiments "in new forms of participatory democracy together with the utopian schemers of a global democracy."[8] Members intentionally contrast themselves with a meeting that takes place on the same days – the World Economic Forum held in Switzerland every year. At the World Economic Forum, leaders discuss international issues, changing markets, and shifting business models. These business leaders assume that systems can be refined and improved, but not entirely replaced.

The World Social Forum makes no such concession when it proclaims the value of alternatives, of the sort that would motivate the most imaginative of science fiction writers. The World Social Forum includes "utopian schemers of a global democracy," thinkers who follow in the tradition of a Renaissance writer who tried to imagine an alternative to the courts of Henry VIII. Sir Thomas More's *Utopia* is sometimes held up as a forerunner of sci-fi since it imagines the perfect society far removed from the corruption of Europe. What policies or governments would actually achieve justice? What happens if society pursues actual morality? Questions for the fantasy writer as much as the politician. The World Social Forum describes itself as "the most recent, vibrant, and potentially productive articulation of an emergent global civil society."[9] The utopian schemers are still here, and still working on the "emergent" society of harmony and justice. When it seems that one model of political exchange dominates, these schemers insist that something other remains: "Through newly exposed cracks in the armor of neoliberal organization, movements are beginning to assert that another world is possible."[10] If one mode of seeing history and especially the history of warfare insists upon necessity, this vision of Utopia embraces possibility and alterity, or otherness. It imagines that "another" way, that an alternative mode, is still out there. "Another world is possible," and humanity can actually reach it.

And the World Social Forum makes a pacifist mission central in its manifesto. "Opposition to war is at the heart of our movement,"[11] it proclaims. Participants are fighting for "An end to war and militarism, foreign military bases and interventions, and the systematic escalation of violence. [They] choose to privilege negotiation and nonviolent conflict resolution."[12] In its pursuit of alternatives, then, the World Social Forum imagines the end of organized violent conflict, a fantasy that may seem laughable to the "hard truth" argument we saw in our introduction. Obama knew violence wouldn't be eradicated any time soon; after all, the history of the world essentially declared the necessity of war. Johan Galtung, however, understood that peace movements depend upon embracing alterity in their visions of the future. He defined the "constructivist" branch of Peace Studies, that field looking to the future for "what *might* work" in contrast to "what *ought* to work."[13] Galtung knows that proposals for peace do not always guarantee success. He also knows that any proposals should be judged against moral or ethical standards. In either case, though, the essential step remains leaving the "hard truths" behind for something like soft fantasies. The imagination embraces possibility and the escape velocity from histories of unrelenting warfare. The World Social Forum states its values with language both powerful and fantastical – and by that we mean fantastical in the best sense. "Another world is possible," they declare, "if based on other values, radically opposed to those that dominate the world today. We cannot forget, however, that the future begins now."[14] That announcement sounds like the stuff of fantasy, but it also sounds like something Galtung would endorse. Embrace what *might* work, for that could be the way to see change through.

It should be no surprise that science fiction welcomes much of the same language. Stories of rockets, androids, and intergalactic travel assume alternatives to the world as-it-is, just as Sir Thomas More used the possibilities of global exploration to conceive his ideal society in *Utopia*. De Witt Douglas Kilgore calls this "astrofuturism": the possibility to look at the frontier of space "as a site of renewal, a place where we can resolve domestic and global battles that have paralyzed our progress on earth."[15] In the explorations of the future lie the potential avenues toward peace, a fantasy especially appealing in the Cold War tensions that drove the space race in the 50s and 60s. Kilgore goes on to analyze the ways in which astrofuturism can adopt and reinforce the imperialistic strains of American history, in which wild lands and people are tamed by the march of American history. Yet in the early moments of the space race, looking beyond the boundaries of Earth allowed "a liberal or utopian commitment that seeks alternatives and solutions to the problems and conflicts characterizing contemporary American life. It can imagine space frontiers predicated on experimental arrangement and the production of relationships uncommon or unknown in the old world."[16] The astrofuturists can judge what might work against what ought to work, and they can do so with the wide-open acres of space.

As the astronauts cross the warp barriers and sail beyond the solar system, they'll bring Shakespeare along with them. He'll be there to witness the utopian commitments of humanity's future. Indeed, he might just make utopia possible.

THE ANDROID'S GUIDE TO SHAKESPEARE

Fans of *Star Trek: The Next Generation* have noticed the literary threads in the television series. Captain Picard — famously played by Patrick Stewart, alum of the Royal Shakespeare Company — loves his Shakespeare. Although he travels throughout the universe in the 24th century, Picard often discovers parallels between Shakespeare's works and the strange new worlds his crew explores. In an episode from the first season titled "Hide and Q," the god-like alien entity Q toys with the *Enterprise*, threatening and tempting the crew in order to test humanity's moral resolve. Q's playful maliciousness is on full display throughout. He dresses as a monk and Napoleonic commander, transports characters without warning through time and space, and pretends to murder the vulnerable crew in violent fashion. His tone changes frequently, and he enjoys the torture like a child torturing insects. Frustrated and desperate, Picard finally confronts Q with a direct question: "Why these games?"[17] The scene takes place in Picard's own chambers, and Q, feet propped up on the desk, has plucked the most relevant of volumes from Picard's shelves: the collected works of Shakespeare (Figure 5.1).

He answers Picard with a snide allusion. "Well, the play is the thing," Q says. "And I'm surprised you have to ask when your human Shakespeare explained it all so well."[18] The exchange is telling. We learn first that Picard does indeed pack Shakespeare when he boards the *Enterprise*. It also appears that alien races know Shakespeare just as well as Earthlings do. In fact, Q puns on the most famous lines from the canon, using the "play's the thing" from *Hamlet* to wink at both Picard's use of "games" and the episode title "Hide and Q."[19] In imagining the future, creator Gene Roddenberry just can't seem to leave out Shakespeare. The playwright guides the show's visions of intergalactic encounter, confrontation, and cooperation.

The same scene of "Hide and Q" jokes with Patrick Stewart's Shakespearean history before it resolves into the idealism typical of *Star Trek*. Always playing with humanity, Q gives

Figure 5.1 Picard knows his stuff ("Hide and Q," *Star Trek: The Next Generation*, Dir. Bowle, Paramount, 1987)

Picard an impromptu test of Shakespearean quotations. Being a starship captain, Picard might not get every allusion, but a member of the RSC will need a steeper challenge:

Q: It's a pity you don't know the content of your own library. Hear this, Picard and reflect: "All the galaxy's a stage [. . .]"

Picard: World, not galaxy – "All the world's a stage."

Q: Oh, you know that one. Well, if he were living now he would have said galaxy. How about this, uh. . . "Life is but a walking shadow, a poor player that struts and frets his hour upon the stage and then is heard

Picard: no more. It is a tale told by an idiot, full of sound and fury, signifying nothing."

Picard: I see. So how we respond to a game tells you more about us than our real life – this "tale told by an idiot."[20]

Q once again puns on the languages of games while engaging in playful banter of his own. His "play" will reveal the truth of humanity better than their real lives. In fact, one could say the same thing of the geek havens of science fiction. The show's winking references to Patrick Stewart and his knowledge of Shakespeare might be frivolous, or it might be the very sort of playfulness that reveals humanity. And that, after all, is speculative fiction – its thought experiments, outlandish "what-if" scenarios, and visions of the future are a test of humanity. Sci-fi writers play their imaginative games to see what humanity ought to do. And in the combination of *Star Trek* and Shakespeare, one conclusion points toward peace.

Picard finishes the scene with an impassioned quotation of his own. When Q threatens Picard with *Hamlet*, Picard fires back, "Oh, I know *Hamlet*, and what he might say with irony I say with conviction: 'What a piece of work is man! How noble in reason. How infinite in faculty. In form, in moving, how express and admirable. In action, how like an angel. In apprehension, how like a god.'"[21] The lines serve not just as a defense of Picard, but of the television series more generally. Q questions the value of humanity, so the captain answers like a sci-fi writer. Picard says, "I see us one day becoming that, Q."[22] Shakespeare is made aspirational, and in that quotation, we might hear Rodenberry speaking to the loftiest ideals of *Star Trek*. In Picard's time, he still hopes for his own future, meaning that the peace work is inevitably ongoing. Turning *Hamlet* into hopefulness – that's the potential in thinking of what ought to be, for television audiences and starship captains alike.

The example of "Hide and Q" is far from the only instance of Shakespeare in Rodenberry's series. According to Elizabeth Baird Hardy, "The most frequently quoted author of the twenty-third and twenty-fourth centuries is undoubtedly William Shakespeare."[23] *Trek* fans and Shakespeareans most often look to the film *Star Trek VI: The Undiscovered Country*. Hamlet's most famous soliloquy is right there in the title, working on a number of levels. It tells us that the film follows in *Star Trek*'s exploration of the "undiscovered" future; it imagines what death might look like for the iconic characters of Kirk and Spock; and it serves as a eulogy for the original franchise reaching its last film. The Shakespeare also doesn't stop there. Allusions and quotations bubble up all throughout the movie, most amusingly in a dinner scene when an alien tells Spock, "You've not experienced Shakespeare until you've read him in the original Klingon."[24] The moment has been analyzed for years by Shakespeareans (a group only made more obsessive when *Star Trek* is added to the mix). Kay H. Smith, for instance, calls it a "Shakespeare gimmick" to have a Klingon captain – played by famous Shakespearean actor Christopher Plummer – "claim the Bard as [his] own cultural property and proceed to quote rings around the bemused officers of the *Enterprise*."[25] As fun as it is, this "gimmick" speaks to the underlying tensions in the plot of *Star Trek VI*. The film begins with declarations of peace; the long-standing wars between the Klingons and the Federation are drawing to a close. It's a thinly veiled allegory for the end of the Cold War. After all, the Berlin wall came down in 1989, only two years before the film was released in 1991. The end of aggression between the two central forces of *Star Trek* invokes anxieties that persist beyond the confines of the film. What happens next? If conflict is over, then what becomes of *Star Trek*'s heroes? And how will old foes integrate into this "undiscovered country"?

Scholar Paul Cantor makes the links between the real-world events of the late 1980s and the Shakespearean allusions of *The Undiscovered Country*. He argues that the film highlights central paradoxes of the series. *Star Trek* prides itself on its egalitarian tolerance, but the prospect of peace also means that the Klingons must abandon the most important aspect of their cultural identity: their belligerence. Tolerance therefore becomes a strange threat that will erase Klingon ways of life. When the writers attach Shakespeare to the Klingons, they threaten the playwright with that same erasure. His plays of war and heroism no longer have a place in the galaxy. They are finally outdated, just like the Klingons.[26] Without his best enemy to battle, Kirk too is made a relic, poignantly banished in one sequence to a frozen tundra. But this reading assumes peace as an ending – the end of heroism, and the end of this future. When Captain Picard picks up his copy of the collected works in *The Next Generation*, he finds new purpose in Shakespeare, and a way to make peace dramatic again. Thankfully, he has a willing audience: an android attempting to comprehend humanity.

A synthetic humanoid named Data emerges as the most important student of Shakespeare in this idealistic vision of the future. The series makes recurrent gags about his desire to understand human emotion, and Patrick Stewart's connections to Shakespeare offer a playful foundation for the captain's role of drama teacher. When Picard made his impassioned speech to Q, he proclaimed his dream that Hamlet's snide remarks on humanity might one day become truth: "What a piece of work is man!" Data's gold skin, discolored eyes, and clipped speech hint at his artificiality, yet Hamlet's speech extends to incorporate this robot. It's not just man who is "infinite in faculty." The android might be too, and the Shakespeare lessons become telling moments of post-human inclusion. Typically, these lessons occur in the Enterprise's holodeck, a playspace in which the crew of a starship can create sets and imaginative scenarios for themselves. These scenes typically revel in the meta-theatrical: The cast of a TV show is allowed to play other characters and suggest that all of theater is equivalent to a holodeck. The Starship Enterprise or the Globe Theater? It doesn't matter. Shakespeare gets his showings.

An episode titled "The Defector" begins with Data on the holodeck, rehearsing the scene of Henry V in which the king secretly visits his troops on the eve of battle. Data gets the best part – that of the king himself. Before Agincourt, Henry hopes to learn the morale of his troops; he also gets the opportunity to express his fears to troops without compromising his position as military leader. Data recites these poignant lines: "I think the king is [. . .] but a man, as I am. The violet smells to him as it doth to me. In his nakedness, he appears but a man."[27] In Henry V, the king insists upon his common humanity. He is afraid of battle just as any soldier would be. When Data gives the lines, he speaks as an android making a plea for humanity. The violet, we can presume, doesn't smell the same to an android as it does to a human, no matter how good the programming. In the middle of this performance, the camera cuts to a pleased-looking Picard, who mouths the words along with the robotic actor. The captain then explains the purpose of this exercise: "Data . . . You're here to learn about the human condition. And there is no better way of doing that than by embracing Shakespeare."[28] One could accuse the series of essentializing human experience to the work of one author from the late 16th century, but the series uses Shakespeare as a proposal for inclusion, to show that definitions of "man" constantly expand. The plot of the episode revolves around a defector from a hostile alien race who boards the *Enterprise*. He warns the crew of a secret Romulan battle station that must be destroyed, and anxieties mount over the course of the hour, putting Picard into the position of *Henry V* on the eve of war. This being *Star Trek: The Next Generation*, missiles are never fired. Instead, the episode ends with ships departing under an uneasy treaty and temporary peace in place. *Star Trek*, it seems, is revising Shakespeare. We begin with the night before the battle at Agincourt; we end without the actual battle. The most martial and heroic of Shakespeare's plays transforms into a lesson for the android, a lesson in the human condition that avoids the violence so often assumed to be natural.

The Shakespearean lessons culminate in "Emergence," an episode from the final season of *Star Trek: The Next Generation*. It begins in the same spot as did "The Defector," in the holodeck. Data continues to perfect his human performances, but the play this time is *The Tempest*, a work we have already seen from the perspective of the pacifist. Data takes on the part of Prospero, caught in the moment of giving up his powers and casting away his books. "I'll break my staff," he bellows from beneath an Elizabethan costume, "bury it certain fathoms in the earth, and deeper than did ever plummet sound I'll [. . .]"[29] Data trails off as he notices that his sole audience member, Picard himself, doesn't listen. Perhaps Picard knows what Data doesn't, that this speech is coming at the end of the show's network television run in 1994. Prospero speaks of the ending to his magic, a moment so often read by Shakespeareans as the playwright's comment on his own impending retirement. This iteration of *Star Trek* is also coming to its end, and breaking its staff (as technologically advanced as that staff might be) before taking its bow. *The Tempest* meditates on endings, punishments, and forgiveness. Here, those themes are recreated in the science fiction setting that allows Shakespeare to speak with hope for ideal futures, even as the episode laments the inevitable conclusion of the narrative. When Data expresses his confusion about Prospero's motivation, Picard offers an explanation: "Shakespeare was witnessing the end of the Renaissance and the birth of the modern era, and Prospero finds himself in a world where his powers are no longer needed. So we see him here about to perform one final creative act before giving up his art forever."[30] Even an android can understand that it's a potentially tragic moment in which the magician – and artist – admits defeat. Picard, though, continues, "there's a certain [. . .] expectancy, too, a hopefulness about the future. You see, Shakespeare enjoyed mixing opposites, the past and the future, hope and despair."[31] He too loses the thought when the performance is interrupted by a speeding train, a sign that the holodeck has malfunctioned. For a moment, though, Picard speaks to the dreams of speculative fiction: Despite the grief at the impending moment of closure, the hopefulness about the future is implicit (Figure 5.2). Other worlds are still possible, and peaceful ones at that.

"Emergence" then moves into a plot with the sort of technological premise familiar to fans of the franchise. The *Enterprise* grows mysterious arrays of circuitry akin to a neural network; indeed, the ship constructs a brain, essentially becoming a creature of free will. In the closing moments of the episode, Data comes back to his Shakespeare. The main

Figure 5.2 Prospero and Picard look to the future ("Emergence," *Star Trek: The Next Generation*, Dir. Bowle, Paramount, 1994)

plot resolves when the sentient Enterprise creates an actual life form, a shiny object made of twisted wires and machinery. It flies out into space, harming nobody. Data notes to Picard, "Captain, you took a substantial risk in allowing the Enterprise to complete its task."[32] The life that grew could have been dangerous; it could have harmed and even destroyed the entire crew. But Picard's tolerance and optimism win out. He maintains a hopefulness for the future that permeates *The Tempest*. Data invites the Captain to a performance of a scene from Shakespeare's play, a scene that audiences well versed in *The Tempest* might expect – the moment Miranda first meets other human beings after her years on the island. Picard finishes the thought for the android: "O brave new world, that has such people in it."³³ The line from Miranda echoes the wondrous quality of her name; she marvels at the possibility of others. The episode closes, then, with an allusion to Shakespeare on not just the possibilities of humanity. It gives a plea for tolerance, peace, and interest. Aldous Huxley might use "O brave new world" cynically, but here, it allows audiences to imagine the future both as Shakespeare saw it and as an android on an intergalactic spaceship might see it. In his analysis of the Shakespearean allusions in this series, David Reinheimer writes, "the optimism of *Star Trek: The Next Generation* grows out of more than the mere presence of Shakespeare or any other historical allusion; rather, the interpretive allusions to Shakespeare demonstrate that our present-day cultures provide in part the very foundation of the Federation."³⁴ In other words, Shakespeare creates the utopian ideal so celebrated in *The Next Generation*. As Harrison knew in "Fragment of a Manuscript," Shakespeare dabbled in his speculative fictions, so it is that Shakespeare offers a pathway to intergalactic peace – no matter if that war has yet to happen. He makes the other world possible.

An advocate of positive peace, scholar Jessica Senehi articulates what she calls "constructive storytelling," a means through which groups can use narratives to understand one another. This form of narrative is "inclusive and fosters collaborative power and mutual recognition; creates opportunities for openness, dialogue, and insight; a means to bring issues to consciousness; and a means of resistance."³⁵ That conception of storytelling is as open-ended and indeterminate as positive peace, and intentionally so. Senehi quotes John Paul Lederach, who responded to 9/11 by telling the story of a high school class that reacted with acceptance and sought out people of Middle Eastern descent. Lederach summed up his intent as any futurist would: "This is a true story except for the parts that haven't happened yet."[36] Positive peace always needs that future. There are always brave new worlds, and we need speculation to get there. That means we're not quite done with Miranda yet, nor her wondering glances.

LIKE WAKING UP FROM A DREAM

Twenty years after the apocalypse, this is not the future of *Star Trek*. Horses drag a stage across a barren landscape, pausing frequently in the blistering heat to rest. To pass the time, their handlers rehearse lines and prepare for the next performance of Shakespeare, as if they are vagabond performers from an earlier era. No androids. No starships. Such is the state of the world in Emily St. John Mandel's 2014 novel *Station Eleven*. Through a series of flashbacks, she flips back and forth between a world at the brink of a catastrophic outbreak and the one crawling out of the wreckage twenty years later. It's hard to read the scene as optimistic, and that's before we learn that these human survivors wear black tattoos of daggers, each recording a murder that occurred somewhere along the way.

St. John Mandel comes back often to a bleak image that seems almost the opposite of *Star Trek*'s gleaming surfaces and lofty astrofuturism. An airplane sits on an abandoned runway, where it first landed during the outbreak of the Georgia flu, the devastating plague that brings about this novel's global catastrophe. Its appearance was ominous enough: "A final plane was landing, an Air Gradia jet, but as Clark watched, it made a slow turn on the tarmac and moved away from instead of toward the terminal building. It parked in the far distance, and no ground crew went to meet it."[37] In that moment, a small number of survivors guess that those inside the airplane knew their fate. They were infected; it was better to quarantine the plane than risk infecting anyone else. So this airplane sits for twenty years, a makeshift coffin for anyone onboard. It is the "ghost plane" (280). We learn that the plane "remained sealed, because opening it was a nightmare no one wanted to think about, because no one knew if the virus could be contracted from the dead, because it was as good a mausoleum as any" (259). In *Station Eleven*, technology gets the survivors to this point – a defeated machine that holds memories we'd rather not know.

Amid this apocalyptic nightmare, however, we find that Shakespeare the pacifist still has a place. Even in the dystopia of St. John Mandel's future, the playwright comes to embody a common humanity. More than that, his plays figure an essential aspect of pointlessness or idleness. They serve no concrete or practical purpose, but it is for that very reason that the performances become models for peacebuilding. They are frivolous, distracting, and fantastical – qualities opposite the hard truths of war. If the grounded plane holds the nightmares of disease and failure, the fantasies of Shakespeare hold promise, pulled by horses from makeshift town to makeshift town. St. John Mandel's grim appropriations of Shakespeare allow human history to emerge anew, not as unending war but as peaceful communalism of the sort that Erasmus proclaimed in the 16th century. What, then, could be more idealistic than an apocalypse?

Approaching dystopia as a hopeful condition perhaps feels like a stretch. These stories so often dwell in the bleakness of death and endings, from Mary Shelley's 19th-century novel *The Last Man*, to Cormac McCarthy's *The Road*, to the latest films of zombie outbreaks or ecological devastation. Critics of the genre have often traced its literary roots to biblical sources, namely, the moment of divine judgment.[38] At the end of the world, we'll find out who and what matters. In Heather Hick's understanding, the rulings extend beyond the individual to the technologies of the modern era: "In text after text, beginning in the Enlightenment period, what has been brought to an apocalyptic end are the physical structures, social formations, and values of modern life, and like the chalk outline of a murder victim, the very absence of these phenomena becomes the primary concern of these narratives."[39] The verdict often doesn't turn out so well, as the collapse of society reveals its fundamental inequality and violence. Think, for instance, of the mystery of soylent green, telling us all how the mechanisms of modernity really work. So the apocalypse gives the world a glimpse of where it's headed; in the words of another writer, the genre shows "how inevitably destructive one possible pathway into the future might be."[40]

Such generalizations are fair, but then so too are the implications that follow. If we stare at the chalk outlines of what collapsed at the moment of judgment, then we are also granted a perverse opportunity to start everything over again, with some imagination and optimism still intact. Gary K. Wolfe, in his take on the post-apocalyptic genre, stresses that potential. Through a number of examples, he emphasizes the re-settlement and survival of humanity, often made in a harmonious relationship with nature or an eye to righting the wrongs of the past. He writes, "it is perhaps most helpful to regard such stories as tales of cosmological displacement: the old concept of 'world' is destroyed and a new one must be built in its place. Economic and political systems, beliefs, and behavior patterns are destroyed, but more often than not the earth abides, and so, at least in part, does humanity."[41] He titles his essay "The Remaking of Zero," a phrase borrowed from J. G. Ballard, a speculative fiction writer who specialized in the apocalypse:

> I believe that the catastrophe story, whoever may tell it, represents a constructive and positive act by the imagination rather than a negative one, an attempt to confront the terrifying void of a patently meaningless universe by challenging it at its own game, to remake zero by provoking it in every conceivable way.[42]

In those terms, blowing up the world is the means to saving the world. The post-apocalyptic novel takes up its place in the literature of peacebuilding, testing the theories of peace ideals and asking about what should be put in place. In that function, this imaginative exercise persists in Johan Galtung's work – it asks that values be put to the test, as if Plato's *Republic* were played out in visions of zombie hoards, collapsing skyscrapers, and vicious plagues.

So *Station Eleven* dwells on images of death only so that it can reassert the values of idealism and Shakespeare. In one sequence, the main character Kirsten Raymonde scavenges in an empty house, looking not so much for supplies as for souvenirs of what's been lost. Her companion August discovers something even better: "He'd found a metal Starship *Enterprise*. He held it up in the sunlight, a gleaming thing the size of a dragonfly" (150). In one sense, this little toy mocks the characters with snide sarcasm. They have entered the future, but they haven't left Earth. But in another sense, the small *Enterprise* anchors the novel in a pervasive hopefulness. Humanity may collapse all around them, but these characters are not so different from the crew of the *Enterprise*. They hold onto that idealism of *The Next Generation*, just in the surprising form of remaking zero. In a later scene, Kirsten suffers a nightmare in which she imagines herself abandoned by all her companions, alone in the post-apocalyptic landscape. She wakes next to August, who gives her the most fitting of comforts. "'I had bad dreams too.' He was holding his silver Starship *Enterprise* in his other hand" (283). The gleaming model protects against those nightmares and inspires hope. Picard, who takes Hamlet's promise for humanity sincerely, would nod in satisfaction. Hold onto the frivolous fantasy; community and salvation depend on it.

If *Star Trek* provides one touchstone for St. John Mandel's novel, Shakespeare provides the other. In the ravaged future, August and Kirsten join with The Traveling Symphony, a group of musicians and actors who entertain the remnants of humanity. St. John Mandel self-consciously picks up the images of pre-modern theater troupes, those medieval groups who would take their shows to audiences, before the theaters were built that would bring audiences to the actors. The makeshift carts of The Traveling Symphony, though, also recall the failed modern era: "The caravans had once been pickup trucks, but now they were pulled by teams of horses on wheels of steel and wood" (36). The pre-modern era has returned, yet the anachronisms remain. This is an early 16th century that strangely features cars, airplanes, and starships – all grimly broken and pointless. The performances regularly feature Shakespeare in yet another sign of what literary critic Philip Smith calls the "forward-backwardness of *Station Eleven*."[43] Even though the novel may be set in the future, the action and characters constantly retreat into the past: "The Symphony performed music – classical, jazz, orchestral arrangements of pre-collapse pop songs – and Shakespeare. They'd performed more modern plays sometimes in the first few years, but what was startling, what no one would have anticipated, was that audiences seemed to prefer Shakespeare to their other theatrical offerings" (37–38). The end of electricity perhaps explains the end of new pop music, but why would audiences want Shakespeare over any other form of drama? The novel lurches backwards and recreates that which had already passed. In those recollections, optimism arises. One actor explains, "People want what was best about the world" (38). Smith sums up the effect well. "The preservation, and continued performance of Shakespeare's works," he writes, "is central to the theme of survival through text. For as long as the characters continue to perform Shakespeare [. . .] something, perhaps all, of civilization survives."[44] The function follows from the novel's time structures. In going back to Shakespeare, the characters recover something of civilization and give their audiences escape from the nightmare of the horrific landscapes. Kirsten woke up from her nightmare to see the small gleaming *Enterprise*. Others wake up to see Shakespeare's performances. One is the other.

When The Traveling Symphony arrives at one particularly forbidding town in the novel's opening chapters, they debate the choice of material. They had planned on *King Lear*, but the mood doesn't seem right. The town is seemingly deserted of the enthusiastic followers that the Symphony had encountered only a couple years before. The choice, then, falls to a comedy when the director declares, "I believe the evening calls for fairies" (44). *A Midsummer Night's Dream* proves most suitable in the barren town, and the director's nod to the fairies implies that fantasy is necessary, something that will help turn the foreboding desertion of the town to humor. St. John Mandel goes on to describe the performance as a moment of light similar to the light that gleams off August's toy *Enterprise*, a flash of something worthwhile among devastation. She writes,

> What was lost in collapse: almost everything, almost everyone, but there is still such beauty. Twilight in the altered world, a performance of *A Midsummer Night's Dream* in a parking lot in the mysteriously named town of St. Deborah by the Water, Lake Michigan shining a half mile away. Kirsten as Titania, a crown of flowers on her close-cropped hair, the jagged scar on her cheekbone half-erased by candlelight.

(57)

Shakespeare substitutes pleasing fantasy for the trauma embodied by the scar on the actor's face. The audience can't see it, only the fantasy. Before the play begins, Kirsten asks her companions about an earlier visit to this location. It seems that townspeople flocked to the actors in appreciation, so Kirsten asks, "I'm not misremembering, am I?" (44). If *Station Eleven* casts humanity back in time, Kirsten's predicament here implies that the past is still up for grabs and that different memories may change the course of the world out of the apocalypse. Shakespeare gives candlelit fantasies in *Midsummer*, a past filled with fantastical fairies and rejuvenating nature, a past that these actors try to recover and implement in their travels. In that effort, they engage in a peaceful journey aimed at bridging communities. So long as they don't misremember.

In fact, the novel opens with a memory lapse. Set during the night that the flu strikes and begins its desolation of humanity, the initial scene begins with *King Lear*, the play that Kirsten and her companions specifically choose to avoid twenty years later. St. John Mandel describes an intriguing staging in which Lear is haunted by hallucinations of three little girls, child actresses who actually play his daughters during a vignette set before the action proper. Speaking to Gloucester, the actor playing Lear recites the line, "I remember thine eyes well enough" (3). Already, the lines and staging foreground recollections of the past, and the effect grows in the next moments. The staging of *King Lear* goes awry when the lead scrambles the next set of lines. He goes back twelve lines and begins saying, "The wren goes to't" (3). Reviewers of the novel note its back and forth structures, especially in a book that "is not so much about apocalypse as about memory and loss, nostalgia and yearning."[45] That pressure on memory starts in the early pages, in a *King Lear* performance that keeps going back to the beginning.

When Kirsten rehearses this play twenty years later, she is also revisiting the past – she was one of the children in the initial performance. She is returning to the losses and heartaches that pervade *King Lear*. St. John Mandel even describes the actors marching along, reciting the same scene with which she begins the novel. It's as if the trauma never ended. This play ends, we know, with Edgar's lament for the suffering of his father's generation: "The oldest hath borne most. We that are young/Shall never see so much, nor live so long" (5.3.300–1). At the beginning of the novel, humanity has already reached one possible end, and the past weighs heavily over younger generations. You can see why Kirsten might want to perform *King Lear* on her tour of the apocalypse, because it embodies the losses and tragedies of her own time. Kirsten does admit, though, that her troupe lacks the right actors. Their Lear, she says, "wasn't really old enough" (36). Since he hasn't "borne most"; it's better to perform *A Midsummers Night's Dream* as a means of remembering something else about humanity – not the invective of Lear calling Goneril "a disease [. . .] a boil,/A plague sore, an embossed carbuncle,/In my corrupted blood" (2.4.217–220). There's been enough disease, even if Kirsten's troupe doesn't have enough years.

The comedy is especially suiting given what the novel's characters know about its initial performance in the 16th century. Kirsten knows that when she recites *A Midsummer Night's Dream*, she speaks "Lines of a play written in 1594, the year London's theaters reopened after two seasons of plague. Or written possibly a year later, in 1595, a year before the death of Shakespeare's only son" (57). *Station Eleven* centers around its own paralyzing disease, the fictional equivalent of the Black Death that swept through Shakespeare's society. Kirsten continues, "Shakespeare was the third born to his parents, but the first to survive infancy. Four of his siblings died young. His son, Hamnet died at eleven and left behind a twin. Plague closed the theaters again and again, death flickering over the landscape" (57). There was no shortage of loss in his time, even to the point of losing his own son. So questions linger about the course of Shakespeare's own life – why bother writing more plays at all? If plague could claim his family at any time, then what's the point of frivolous entertainment? That charge of futility belies Peace Studies as well. If the history of humanity is endless, unavoidable war, then what's the point of trying something else? Isn't peacebuilding just a frivolous fantasy distracting from the practical work of the real world? The novel offers answers to those questions by perfectly blending Shakespeare with the idealism of *Star Trek*. A single phrase is written across the lead wagon of The Traveling Symphony: "*Because survival is insufficient*" (58). Kirsten keeps the same line tattooed on her forearm, and she does admit its origins. She cribbed it from an episode of *Star Trek: Voyager*, yet another series imagining a distant utopian future. Shakespeare becomes the stuff of *Star Trek*; the time is right for fairies because survival is insufficient. If these characters are going to repeat human history, if they are going to start over from the point of nothingness, they have the opportunity to create an alternate past in which violence isn't justified by the amoral refrain, "I did it because I had to survive." The actor Dieter can't see the profundity, instead attacking the *Star Trek* line as below the dignity of this theatrical company. This is the "whole problem," he says. "The best Shakespearean actress in the territory, and her favorite line of text is from *Star Trek*" (120). Without realizing, Kirsten gives the perfect response in the form of a question: "The whole problem with what?" (120). She has abandoned pretense and married the premodernity of Shakespeare to the fantastical sci-fi of *Star Trek*. In fact, as she responds to Dieter, she feels "that she might actually be dreaming" (120), as if she enters into the spaces of *A Midsummer Night's Dream*. These performers instead learn to endure with art and fantasy – the sort of pointlessness that can produce peace. If anyone asks why they waste time performing early modern plays amid the apocalypse, the answer is painted on the side of the lead truck.

King Lear and *A Midsummer Night's Dream* provide two opposite reactions to the apocalypse, but a third play waits just under the surface of St. John Mandel's novel. In a series of flashbacks set before the apocalypse, we come to know the first wife of a famous Hollywood actor Arthur Leander, the very same actor who dies playing Lear in the opening pages. Data would certainly get the reference in his wife's name – Miranda. In *Star Trek: The Next Generation*, Data uses her line "brave new world" as a promise of future tolerance and collaboration. In *Station Eleven*,

Miranda first appears as a dreamer without clear purpose in life. The actor Arthur first meets her because they share the same hometown, not insignificantly a hometown isolated on an island. The Delano Island is "all temperate rain forest and rocky beaches," where children "go barefoot all summer and wear feathers in their hair" (73). *The Tempest* again. Miranda of *Station Eleven*, a child of an island just like her Shakespearean counterpart, stands out for a graphic novel that she is constantly writing and that ends up in the hands of Kirsten in the post-apocalyptic narrative. This novel-within-the-novel has the complicated plot of the best speculative fiction: The hero Dr. Eleven fled Earth after a race of hostile aliens attacked, and he has flown a planet-sized spaceship named *Station Eleven* through a wormhole to escape. Now, he floats in the deep reaches on a flooded planet-ship, living on scattered islands. All of this in a graphic novel that St. John Mandel describes second-hand. The oceans and castaway elements recall *The Tempest*, but also telling are the reactions of others to Miranda's art project. One boyfriend accusingly asks Miranda about how she fills her days at a slow job, "And what do you do in that *downtime*, Miranda?" (84). She works on this project, composed of beautiful paintings that ruminate on apocalypse and loss. It has no immediate purpose, but Miranda admits, "Station Eleven will be my constant" (89). Shakespeare's son died at age 11, the number echoing in Miranda's work. If *A Midsummer Night's Dream* shouted back at the desolation of plague and death with fantasy, so does Miranda's project insist on its own importance, precisely because it's unimportant.

That value appears in a dinner party scene that also takes place before the flu wipes out humanity. St. John Mandel describes the dinner in terms of *The Tempest*. Miranda "is marooned on a strange planet" (92) and the party itself a "shipwreck" (99). She is, like the characters she writes, stuck in limbo. Conversation turns to the subject of her graphic novel. "What do you plan to do with it once it's done?" (94), one guest asks her. She answers, "I don't know" (94) and shrugs off suggestions that she publish it. Miranda explains, "It makes me happy. It's peaceful, spending hours working on it. It doesn't really matter to me if anyone else sees it" (95). She may as well say, "Because survival is insufficient." She seeks only the paradoxical idleness of "working on it," meaning that her work frustrates conceptions of profit and utility. At a later moment, her ex-husband Arthur reveals his inability to comprehend Miranda's attitude when he says, "I never really understood the point of it, to be honest" (320). By looking for "the point of it," he misses the peacefulness inherent to her project. He cannot understand the idleness as dreaming or as memory, nor the value in seeing her hours working on it as the end in and of itself.

Even the content of Miranda's writing pleads for creative resolution to seemingly hopeless conflict. The Miranda of *The Tempest* is the one to say, "O wonder!/How many goodly creatures are there here!/How beauteous mankind is! O brave new world/That has such people in't!" (5.1.184–87). With hints of the same optimism, the Miranda of *Station Eleven* sees the beauty in the villains of her novel-within-the-novel, characters called the Undersea who try to steer Dr. Eleven back to Earth. St. John Mandel describes the changes: "For years Dr. Eleven had been the hero of the narrative, but lately he'd begun to annoy her and she'd become more interested in the Undersea. These people living out their lives in underwater fallout shelters, clinging to the hope that the world they remembered could be restored" (213). She grows sympathy, and the demarcations of conflict shift. In that, Miranda frustrates conventional narrative logic and writes a story without conclusion. If someone doesn't understand the point, they're looking for the wrong sorts of stories, the kind that end conflict with only more violence. The limbo will continue in Miranda's "never-ending project" (82) – as will the peacefulness of spinning out their story.

In *The Tempest*, Shakespeare's Miranda does not quite know how she wound up on the island. Prospero must tell her the story of how he was betrayed, forced from his dukedom by his own brother with a "treacherous army" (1.2.128) behind him. Prospero, of course, uses violence himself, most troublingly in his treatment of Caliban and the sprite Ariel. Miranda's reaction, though, is one of innocence. When Prospero asks what she knows of the time before the island, she answers, "'Tis far off,/And rather like a dream than an assurance/ That my remembrance warrants" (1.2.44–46). That response blends dreaming into memory, leaving Prospero with the opportunity to craft her recollections just as he magically affects the dreams of the sailors who crash on his island. Miranda's wondering response shows up in *Station Eleven*, but more often in the mind of Kirsten. This actress wanders the decimated landscape of the United States, but curiously, she has no memory of the year that followed the flu. Indeed, the gaps are everywhere. "I have some problems with memory," Kirsten says. "I can't remember very much from before the collapse" (113). All has been erased by a mind unwilling to deal with the trauma. But the specific echo of Miranda comes when Kirsten says, "My memories from before the collapse seem like dreams now" (195). The past is uncertain and foreboding, a dream one might not want to recall. Kirsten mentions a brother who fled with her in that first lost year. She knows that "her brother had been plagued by nightmares"

(304), and when she asks, he says "I hope you never remember it" (304). Nightmares, like the plane sitting on the runway, are better left sealed.

Prospero speaks another line on dreams, this one far more familiar to Shakespeare fans. It comes when he stops the pageant of spirits, moments before breaking his staff and giving up his magic: "We are such stuff/As dreams are made on, and our little life/Is rounded with a sleep" (4.1.156–158). That sober reflection casts life as the fantasy, the spectacle to be witnessed only in passing. It also casts human activity as momentary, perhaps purposeless. At the end of this poignant reflection, Miranda leaves the scene with Ferdinand, speaking an innocuous goodbye: "We wish your peace" (4.1.163). When these scenes are played in *Star Trek: The Next Generation*, Picard comments on the mixed modes, that Shakespeare gives moments of grief and hope together. The final scenes of *The Tempest* let go and indulge forgiveness. Traumatic dreams end, and peacefulness ensues. Prospero tells his former enemies, "Let us not burden our remembrance with/A heaviness that's gone" (5.1.202–203). If dreams and memories blend, Shakespeare here gives the possibility of release from nightmares and the embrace of the sort of magic that can revise trauma.

These notions of memory, fantasy, and hope arise in some of the most unexpected moments in *Station Eleven*. That novel's Miranda never makes it past Armageddon; instead, she dies on a beach as the plague overtakes the world. Her demise, though, brings with it a remarkable beauty that echoes the performance of *A Midsummer Night's Dream* at twilight, with sparkling water in the background. In a delirious haze and looking over the ocean, the dying Miranda sees the sunrise in "pink and streaks of brilliant orange, the container ships on the horizon suspended between the blaze of the sky and the water aflame, the seascape bleeding into confused visions of the spacecraft called Station Eleven, its extravagant sunsets and its indigo sea. The light of the fleet fading into morning, the ocean burning into sky" (228). Her vision merges with her art, and one wonders what is the dream, what is reality. At the end of St. John Mandel's novel, we do get final lines from the graphic novel, a bit of dialogue between Dr. Eleven and a ghost named Lonagam:

Dr. Eleven: What was it like for you, at the end?
Captain Lonagam: It was exactly like waking up from a dream.
(330)

Death transforms to another beginning, and we can see the constructive purposes in the post-apocalyptic novel. Through these elaborate descriptions, speculative plots, and Shakespearean allusions, St. John Mandel gives new visions and new memories. Her characters and readers wake up from a dream, into a world unburdened by the heaviness of memory or the traumatic nightmares that replay – and defend – violence.

The characters of *The Tempest* aren't the only ones in Shakespeare who wake up from dreams. Not to state the obvious, but dreams also play their part *A Midsummer Night's Dream*, which we've already shown concludes with simultaneous pleas for fellowship and frivolity. In the middle, Oberon gives instructions to Puck: Put the humans back to sleep and "When they next wake, all this derision/Shall seem a dream and fruitless vision" (3.2.371–372). At the moment of waking up, once the confusions of the plot are resolved, "all things shall be peace" (3.2.378). The dream gets them there. In *Station Eleven*, that same language of dreaming works toward peaceful resolution. The traumatic memories of the apocalypse will be forgotten, and Kirsten will discover a world ready for peace. This world looks like Shakespeare's – cast back into the past – but with potential for creative resolution and peaceful pointlessness.

One of the actors in The Traveling Symphony, called only "the clarinet," is less sold on the value of Shakespeare. In fact, "the clarinet hated Shakespeare" (288). She has heard all the comparisons, that "Shakespeare had lived in a plague-ridden society with no electricity and so did the Traveling Symphony" (288). It doesn't help. She says, "In Shakespeare's time the wonders of technology were still ahead, not behind them" (288). She refuses to embrace the anachronism of St. John Mandel's conceit. *Station Eleven* depends upon a world being cast backward in time, with the possibility for revising the past. It depends upon a curious inversion of the World Social Forum: Another World Was Possible. That is, another version of humanity could have existed, defined not by "practical" violence or the "hard truth" of war, but by the frivolity of the fantastical.

Kirsten doesn't remember the past, but her oblivion works to her advantage. One child of the apocalypse defends violence, telling Kirsten, "What choice do I have? You know this time [. . .] this time we live in, you know how it forces a person to do things" (292). That is the defense of a "realist" committing violence. One of Kirsten's companions responds not with alternate futures, but with alternate pasts: "That seems a strange statement [. . .] coming from someone too young to remember any different" (292). And that's what the speculative use of Shakespeare does – it lets you remember differently. From a different past comes the different future; they are one and the same. In the final moments of the novel, lights appear for the first time in the post-apocalyptic age. We first see them through the eyes of Clark, who describes the future invention of electricity in terms of the utopian idealist. He asks himself, "If there are again towns with streetlights, if there are symphonies and newspapers, then what else might this awakening world contain?" (332). The world wakes up from a dream, and as Oberon says, "all things shall be peace." The end inspires a new history of the world. Humanity is given a chance to remember that another world was possible.

In this book's introduction, we saw Obama's grim view of human history: "War, in one form or another, appeared with the first man. At the dawn of history, its morality was not questioned; it was simply a fact, like drought or disease [. . .]" The simplicity of fact is devastating. That "dawn of history" justifies war in both the present and future; after all, if war appeared with the first man, unquestioned in its morality, then how would humanity ever expect anything different. Another world is possible? Only if you ignore the violence that gave birth to this world.

Sci-fi Shakespeares imagine the altered world. Although *Station Eleven* may envision a grim landscape in which violence traumatizes its characters, it also resets the clock, like the best of post-apocalyptic narratives. This is not to ignore the very real trauma of war or genocide in the past; it instead offers the narrative to rethink how we got here. St. John Mandel reads like a 21st-century Erasmus. After all, he was the one to write, "[I]f we consider just the condition and appearance of the human body, is it not apparent at once that Nature, or rather God, created this animal not for war but for friendship, not for destruction but for preservation, not for aggression but to be helpful?"[46] The violence of past memory fades. Another world was possible, one that has already had its Shakespeare and the unimportant stuff that makes peace.

NOTES

1 Harry Harrison, "A fragment of a manuscript," in *Microcosmic Tales*, ed. Isaac Asimov, Martin H. Greenberg, and Joseph D. Olander (New York: Daw Books, Inc., 1980), 269–71, 269.

2 Ibid.

3 Harrison, "A fragment of a manuscript," 270.

4 Ibid.

5 Ibid., 271.

6 Ibid.

7 Peter Y. Paik, *From Utopia to Apocalypse: Science Fiction and the Politics of Catastrophe* (Minneapolis: University of Minnesota Press, 2010), 2.

8 Michael Hardt and Antonio Negri, "Foreword," in *Another World is Possible: World Social Forum Proposals for an Alternative Globalization*, ed. William F. Fisher and Thomas Ponniah (London: Zed Books, 2003), xxvi.

9 Thomas Ponniah and William F. Fisher, "Introduction: The world social forum and the reinvention of democracy," in *Another World is Possible: World Social Forum Proposals for an Alternative Globalization*, ed. William F. Fisher and Thomas Ponniah (London: Zed Books, 2003), 1.

10 Ibid.

11 "Epilogue: Social movements' manifesto," in *Another World is Possible: World Social Forum Proposals for an Alternative Globalization*, ed. William F. Fisher and Thomas Ponniah (London: Zed Books, 2003), 347.

12 Ibid., 351.

13 Johan Galtung, *Peace by Peaceful Means: Peace and Conflict: Development and Civilization* (London, Thousand Oaks, and New Delhi: SAGE Publications, 1996), 11. The emphasis is ours.

14 Michael Löwy and Frei Betto, "Values of a new civilization," trans. Robert Finnegan and Thomas Ponniah, in *Another World is Possible: World Social Forum Proposals for an Alternative Globalization*, ed. William F. Fisher and Thomas Ponniah (London: Zed Books, 2003), 337.

15 De Witt Douglas Kilgore, *Astrofuturism: Science, Race, and Visions of Utopia in Space* (Philadelphia: University of Pennsylvania Press, 2003), 2.

16 Ibid., 4.

17 C. J. Holland and Gene Roddenberry, "Hide and Q," *Star Trek: The Next Generation* (1987), digital video.

18 Ibid.

19 Shakespeare's appearance in *The Next Generation* does mark a stark difference from the original series, as witnessed in the episode of *Star Trek* titled "The Conscience of the King." This episode features a murderous fugitive using a Shakespearean troupe as cover to escape justice. Because Kirk uncovers the deception but decides not to execute the villain, he brings the episode to less tragic conclusions. Mary Buhl Dutta, in "'Very Bad Poetry, Captain': Shakespeare in 'Star Trek,'" *Extrapolation* 36.1 (1995), digital text, calls Kirk "the new Shakespearean hero, possessor of the enlightened values of the future." *The Next Generation* does not merely "solve" the problems of Shakespeare's violence but turns the playwright into a valuable guide for pacifism.

20 Ibid.

21 Ibid.

22 Ibid.

23 Elizabeth Bair Hardy, "Shakespeare (and the rest of the great books) in the original Klingon," in *Star Trek and History*, ed. Nancy C. Reagin (Hoboken: Wiley, 2013), 181.

24 Nicholas Meyer, dir., *Star Trek VI: The Undiscovered Country* (1991), digital video.

25 Kay H. Smith, "'Hamlet, Part Eight, The Revenge' or Sampling Shakespeare in a Postmodern World," *College Literature* 31.4 (2004): 135–49, 140.

26 See Paul Cantor, "Shakespeare in the Original Klingon: Star Trek and the End of History," *Perspectives on Political Science* 29.3 (2000): 158–66.

27 Ronald D. Moore, "The Defector," *Star Trek: The Next Generation* (1990), digital video.

28 Ibid.

29 Joe Menosky and Brannon Braga, "Emergence," *Star Trek: The Next Generation* (1994), digital video.

30 Ibid.

31 Ibid.

32 Ibid.

33 Ibid.

34 David Reinheimer, "Ontological and Ethical Allusion: Shakespeare in 'The Next Generation,'" *Extrapolation* 36.1 (1995), digital text.

35 Jessica Senehi, "Constructive Storytelling: A Peace Process," *Peace and Conflict Studies* 9.2 (2002): 41–63, 45.

36 Ibid., 57.
37 Emily St. John Mandel, *Station Eleven* (New York: Vintage Books, 2014), 236. All subsequent references to this edition will be cited within the text.
38 See for example David J. Leigh, *Apocalyptic Patterns in the Twentieth-Century Fiction* (Notre Dame: Notre Dame Press, 2008).
39 Heather J. Hicks, *The Post-Apocalyptic Novel in the Twenty-First Century: Modernity Beyond the Salvage* (New York: Palgrave Macmillan, 2016), 4.
40 Frederik Pohl, "The politics of prophecy," in *Political Science Fiction*, ed. Donald M. Hassler and Clyde Wilcox (Columbia: University of South Carolina Press, 1997), 9.
41 Gary K. Wolfe, *Evaporating Genres: Essays on Fantastic Literature* (Middletown: Wesleyan University Press, 2011), 86.
42 Quoted in Wolfe, *Evaporating Genres*, 88.
43 Philip Smith, "Shakespeare, Survival, and the Seeds of Civilization in Emily St. John Mandel's Station Eleven," *Extrapolation* 57.3 (2016): 289–303, 301.
44 Ibid., 297.
45 Justine Jordan, "Flu wipes out 99% of humanity in a hotly tipped novel about memory, art and survival: Station Eleven by Emily St John Mandel," *The Guardian* (London), September 27, 2014. Philip Smith also observes the shuffled lines of Lear: "the performance of King Lear appears to bring forth the apocalypse it describes. In this moment we are presented with a microcosm of the post-apocalyptic genre; the simultaneous movement forward and back encircling the moment of Armageddon" (290).
46 Desiderius Erasmus, "Dulce bellum inexpertis," in *Collected Works of Erasmus: Adages III.iv 1 to IV ii 100*, vol. 35, ed. John N. Grant, trans. Denis L. Drysdall (Toronto: University of Toronto Press, 2001), 399–440, 401.

Afterword

War is not the answer

This book began with Julius Caesar in a long red tie, his blond coif an unmistakable signal to the audience. If power transferred peacefully to Donald Trump in the 2016 American election, the New York summer production of Shakespeare's play only months later envisioned his violent assassination in the effort to protect republican ideals and change the course of history. The controversy that followed spoke not just to the divisiveness of American politics but also to the ongoing potential of theater. *Julius Caesar* could still shock. A play could still drive social action. In one February afternoon of 1601, Shakespeare's company performed *The Killing of King Richard the Second*, and on the next day, the Earl of Essex led an uprising through London that challenged the power of Elizabeth and her court.[1] It wasn't a coincidence: Certain followers of Essex had specifically requested the performance at the Globe. For people living in Shakespeare's day, the theater was clearly an explosive place with real political impact. In Central Park hundreds of years later, a few lines of blank verse seemed to have that same potential.

So that summer's production of *Julius Caesar* in 2016 wasn't the first time one of Shakespeare's plays was interpreted as speaking to contemporary fantasies of political assassination. We see another instance in 1967, when the Village Gate Theater staged Barbara Garson's *MacBird*, a satirical take on *Macbeth*.

The condemnations came swiftly. Tom Prideaux's review in *Life* magazine ran with the title "A Satire Strictly for the Macbirds," and he didn't hold back: "Barbara Garson obviously had a high old time with her nutty and cruel accusations, but they can hardly be taken seriously as astute political satire."[2] The *New York Times* critic Walter Kerr called the play "tasteless and irresponsible."[3] One other unexpected critic also saw the inevitable dangers of political Shakespeare; J. Edgar Hoover censured *MacBird* in his monthly *Law Enforcement Bulletin* for the FBI.[4] The problem? The play recast Lyndon B. Johnson as an American Macbeth, a politician who seizes the throne by orchestrating the assassination of his king, John F. Kennedy. If casting Trump as Julius Caesar bothered some, so did turning JFK into Duncan and LBJ into the most notorious of the playwright's criminals. This Shakespeare, it seems, was just too cruel and irresponsible for the Vietnam era.

When Garson began *MacBird* in 1966, she partook in the protest movements of the time. Her idea for an LBJ-themed *Macbeth* took shape at an anti-war rally in Berkeley, where the pacifist motivations were immediate. Garson mistakenly called LBJ's wife "Lady MacBird Johnson," and so Shakespeare emerged as a pacifist for the 1960s.[5] The moment was appropriate. According to Tom Blackburn, on the day *MacBird* opened, "*The Times* reported that US casualties [in Vietnam] were the war's highest, with 144 killed, 1044 wounded, and six missing."[6] Garson's anger toward the war shows in the viciousness with which she satirizes not just LBJ but the entirety of the political establishment, including the Kennedy family and the Democratic Party. All participate in and perpetuate the violence of American empire, and Shakespeare proves the best voice with which to call them out.

When we hear Shakespeare's voice come through in the play, we hear anti-war protestors denouncing the callousness of American policy. Once MacBird takes the Oval Office, a reporter asks for his thoughts on Vietnam. MacBird responds, "Where is this Viet Land? Who gave them folks permission to rebel?"[7] His ignorance quickly shifts to belligerence:

> Since when do we permit an open challenge
> To all the world's security and peace?
> Rip out those Reds! Destroy them, root and branch!
> Deploy whatever force you think we need!
> Eradicate this noxious, spreading weed![8]

"MacNamara" answers with appropriate Shakespearean language as he agrees, "that land will be subdued ere set of sun."[9] The play may have started as a slip-of-the-tongue at an anti-war rally, but it turned into an extended protest, a critique of the narrative that fueled the Vietnam War. How could a Communist force challenge the world order? Best to destroy them in the name of preserving peace.

Garson's strongest critiques come through the three witches, represented in MacBird by three counter-cultural icons. It is an "old leftist" who takes up the subject of Vietnam in a satirical version of the witches' chant:

> Taylor's tongue and Goldberg's slime,
> MacNamara's bloody crime
> Sizzling skin of a napalmed child,
> Now we add a fiery chunk
> From a burning Buddhist monk.[10]

The meter echoes Shakespeare's, and we get a Vietnam era image of the war's crimes cooked into the cauldron. As the ingredients of political dissent mix, the witches together speak the famous lines of *Macbeth*, with slogans lifted from the 1965 Watts riots. They say, "Bubble and bubble, toil and trouble, *Burn baby burn*, and cauldron bubble."[11] Shakespeare blends with 1960s protests as they weave into his rhymes and meter.

It's easy, then, for Garson to discover the beatnik in Shakespeare, to read *Macbeth* at the war protest. Macbeth's violence is just the personal ambition, greed, and bloodlust that motivates the wide-scale violence of the Vietnam War. Macbeth sees a dagger appear before him; so does the American politician see a version of his own tempting dagger when he is eager to destroy in the name of peace.

Garson's insights find a surprising echo in the politics of the early 2000s. Karl Rove, the policy advisor and Deputy Chief of Staff for George W. Bush, is often credited with helping Bush to electoral victory, but Rove also takes his learning from the Renaissance. In a podcast hosted by Stephen Dubner of *Freakonomics*, Rove explains,

> The best course that I ever took in college was in my sophomore year, and it was a course in Shakespearean literature. I learned more about political communications in that one semester from a Catholic nun than I learned in any political science course. It made me aware of the power of language, and how telling a story . . . a political campaign is about big issues, but you have to describe a narrative. You have to create a storyline.[12]

While Rove may not have directly led the invasions of Iraq and Afghanistan, he orchestrated the campaigns that made them possible. It was narrative power, he says, that produced a sense of rational logic and inevitability. One can recognize that the same narratives that make a run for office possible can also make war possible. Shakespeare gave Rove political communication, and from that follows the narratives of ongoing violent conflict.[13] But Shakespeare can also give the alternatives. As we have shown throughout this book, he gives us storylines that don't simply end in peace. Many of this plays make peace itself the storyline.

When Trump won the U.S. presidential election in 2016, he pronounced a narrative of his own, one that seized upon American history with terms of nostalgia and restoration. It can be seen in the campaign slogan he embroidered on countless red hats: "Make America Great Again." When it comes to foreign policy or national defense, this call to history is distinctly militaristic. Trump follows in the seduction outlined by Andrew Bacevich that we quoted in the introduction. The notion that "Americans have come to define the nation's strength and well-being in terms of military preparedness" makes the connection obvious in its public promises: "President Donald J. Trump will Make the American Military Great Again."[14] That act of recollection involves increased spending, bolstering recruitment, and rebuilding the American nuclear arsenal. It's not hard to see that Trump invokes a particular past that has largely guided the narrative of American foreign policy after 1945. In the language of the White House itself, "Rebuilding U.S. deterrence to preserve peace through strength must be our Nation's top priority. The unprecedented era of peace that followed World War II revealed that the free world is safest when America is strongest."[15] In this account, the Korean War, the Cold War, and the Vietnam War all together form an "unprecedented era of peace." It's the sort of peace that can come only from direct military action.

In his own speeches, Trump turns to the familiar refrains of *Coriolanus*: War is practical, realistic, and active. It's all too easy to denounce peace as "a very apoplexy, lethargy; mulled, deaf, sleepy, insensible." It's the "nothing" that seems so threatening to the warriors of *Much Ado About Nothing*. In a speech to a conservative political group shortly after his victory, Trump bemoaned the wars that he inherited from Obama and Bush. "The era of empty talk is over," he said. "Now is the time for action."[16] The action includes "one of the greatest military buildups in American history," an act of aggression that means "Nobody will dare question our military might again."[17] Peace demands strength; it demands prolonged acts of violence. Otherwise, idleness and weakness take over, leading the enemies of the world to question "military might again." The contradiction is once again here – to keep war from breaking out, you pursue war.

In the same speech, Trump phrased his strategy as a moment of arousal. He announced, "we are calling for a great reawakening of America, a resurgence of confidence, and a rebirth of patriotism, prosperity, and pride."[18] He used the same rhetoric in a speech to the U.N., a talk in which he threatened North Korea with total devastation. Trump explains, "One of the greatest American patriots, John Adams, wrote that the American Revolution was 'effected before the war commenced. The Revolution was in the minds and hearts of the people.' That was the moment when America awoke, when we looked around and understood that we were a nation."[19] If military buildup amounts to action, then so does initiating wars count as waking up. That's the impetus in the recollection of a certain kind of history, and in calling the era following World War II an era of peace. It's counted as waking up, rejecting supposed weakness and reclaiming military strength. No dreaming here and, certainly, no perceived idleness that comes with peace.

Coriolanus would say the same. But then, he never experienced the dream visions of *Cymbeline*, *A Midsummer Night's Dream*, or *The Tempest*. There, we can find the alternate political narratives to endless war.

Recall that at the end of *Cymbeline*, war is indeed resolved between Britain and Rome, and Posthumus' future seems secure. Shakespeare delights in the anachronisms, as if he were one of the speculative fiction writers we saw before. The final lines of this play usher in the characters' future, but they also cast an alternative past for Shakespeare's England. "Never was a war did cease," Cymbeline says, "Ere bloody hands were washed, with such a peace" (5.6.484–485). In the conceit of the play, the hands are already washed, and peace is here for Britain. Posthumus wakes up, alongside Shakespeare's audience, to pacifism. Given how Karl Rove looks to Shakespeare for political communication and the language to direct actual policy, he would also do well to find the values in the dreams and seeming frivolity of nothingness. The dagger isn't always hanging in the air, no matter how much Coriolanus, MacBird, or Trump might want it to be. We should always remember that Macbeth sees the dagger "before" him, an ambiguous term that leaves open whether his past must determine the direction of his future.

Macbeth could just go to bed and possibly to more pleasant dreams. He could take a beat, slow down, and embrace the conflict inherent in the idle moment. And, in choosing instead to dream, he would join so many of the pacifists we have heard from in this volume: Data, Gbowee, Ginsberg, Gonzalo, Lennon, Miranda, Puck, Rosalind, and Touchstone. Instead of seeing violence as a solution, Macbeth could realize that war *is not the answer*. That familiar peace slogan appears in Marvin Gaye's protest song "What's Going On" (1971), where the title at first seems to refer to the soldiers dying, picket signs, and brutality that the singer sees all around him. However, as the song progresses, we realize that Gaye wants to offer us a different story about "what's going on." He wants to let us know that "We don't need to escalate/You see, war is not the answer/For only love can conquer hate."[20] In retrospect, the song becomes the promise of another narrative where the time of trouble reveals the senselessness of violent conflict and the need to build a new world while we embrace new ways of being. There is plenty "going on" when we choose answers other than war. We can recast peace as the star of real-world and fictional drama. We can see peace as the interesting stuff. We can then ask for more.

NOTES

1 Quoted in Paul E. J. Hammer, "Shakespeare's Rising, the Play of 7 February 1601, and the Essex Rising," *Shakespeare Quarterly* 59.1 (2008): 1–35, 1. Hammer examines whether the exact play was Shakespeare's *Richard II*.

2 Tom Prideaux, "A Satire Strictly for the Macbirds," *Life* (March, 1967): 16.

3 Quoted in Bruce E. Altschuler, "Macbeth and political corruption," in *Shakespeare and Politics*, ed. Bruce E. Altschuler and Michael A Genovese (New York: Routledge, 2016), 27–47, 38.

4 Ibid., 38.

5 Tom Blackburn recounts these origins in "MacBird! And Macbeth: Topicality and Imitation in Barbara Garson's Satirical Pastiche," *Shakespeare Survey* 57 (2004): 137–44, 138.

6 Ibid., 138.

7 Barbara Garson, *MacBird* (Berkeley and New York: Grassy Knoll Press, 1966), 28.

8 Ibid., 28.

9 Ibid., 28.

10 Ibid., 41.

11 Ibid., 41.
12 "Freakonomics Goes to College, Part I: Full Transcript," *Freakonomics*, July 30, 2012, http://freakonomics.com/2012/07/30/freakonomics-goes-to-college-part-1-full-transcript/
13 In *Society Must Be Defended*, Michel Foucault asks, "What is the exercise of power?" In order to answer his question, he pursues a year-long set of lectures on the notion that power "is war, the continuation of war by other means" (15). He reverses Clausewitz's classic formulation and suggests, "Politics is the continuation of war by other means." Such a meditation is not just the stuff of high-minded theory. The book shows up on President Bartlett's bookshelf on the final episode of *The West Wing*, suggesting we should take seriously the purchase of Foucault's ideas on contemporary politics.
14 "President Donald J. Trump will Make the American Military Great Again," *The White House*, December 12, 2017, www.whitehouse.gov/briefings-statements/president-donald-j-trump-will-make-american-military-great/
15 "National Security & Defense," *The White House*, www.whitehouse.gov/issues/national-security-defense/page/4/, accessed January 2018
16 "Remarks by President Trump at the Conservative Political Action Conference," *The White House*, February 24, 2017, www.whitehouse.gov/briefings-statements/remarks-president-trump-conservative-political-action-conference/
17 Ibid.
18 "Remarks by President Trump on the Strategy in Afghanistan and South Asia," *The White House*, August 21, 2017, https://www.whitehouse.gov/briefings-statements/remarks-president-trump-strategy-afghanistan-south-asia/
19 "Remarks by President Trump to the 72nd Session of the United Nations General Assembly," *The White House*, September 19, 2017, www.whitehouse.gov/briefings-statements/remarks-president-trump-72nd-session-united-nations-general-assembly/
20 Marvin Gaye, "What's Going On" (Tamla, 1971).

Further reading

Many excellent studies can help illuminate themes of pacifism in Shakespeare's work and in the Renaissance more broadly. Several notable discussions of peace occur in the context of larger examinations of martial conflict and culture. An excellent starting place for understanding the role of war in early modern drama is Patricia Cahill's *Unto the Breach: Martial Formations, Historical Trauma, and the Early Modern Stage* (Oxford: Oxford University Press, 2009), which considers how Shakespeare, Marlowe, and their contemporaries staged military scenes in the context of the early modern audience's political moment. Curtis C. Breight's *Surveillance, Militarism and Drama in the Elizabethan Era* (New York: Palgrave Macmillan, 1996) more specifically scrutinizes how Marlowe and Shakespeare's dramas represent the political factions in Renaissance England that instigated national and international violence. In *1590s Drama and Militarism: Portrayals of War in Marlowe, Chapman, and Shakespeare's Henry V* (Burlington: Ashgate, 2001), Nina Taunton traces how literary and nonliterary texts – plays by Shakespeare and Marlowe, as well as military manuals and correspondence – captured the military's unease in the last few years of Elizabeth I's reign. Paola Pugliatti's *Shakespeare and the Just War Tradition* (Burlington: Ashgate, 2010) explores the representation of war in Shakespeare's plays and the concept of a "just war" that abounded in the literature and culture of Elizabethan England. Nick De

Somogyi's provocative *Shakespeare's Theatre of War* (Burlington: Ashgate, 1994) draws parallels between war and theater, concluding his study with an in-depth investigation of *Hamlet*. Two other general studies in the same vein are Oliver Ford Davies and James Pettifer's *God Keep Lead Out of Me: Shakespeare on War and Peace* (Stratford-Upon-Avon: Royal Shakespeare Company, 1985) and Peter Milward's essay "War and Peace in Shakespeare," *Religion and Arts* 11.2, 2007. One notable exception to the trend to pair Shakespeare with war is the article "Shakespeare's Pacifism," *Renaissance Quarterly* 45.1, 1992, where Steven Marx maps Shakespeare's transformation from an advocate for war to one for peace as he reflects England's changing outlook on foreign policy.

Another evocative line of inquiry into Shakespeare's pacifism involves considering how his work has been performed in the context of modern wars. The collection of essays in *Shakespeare and War* (New York: Palgrave Macmillan, 2008), ed. Paul Franssen and Ros King, ranges in subject from Shakespeare's reading of war manuals written by a mercenary to how Nazi Germany, wartime Denmark, and Cold War Romania staged Shakespeare's works. In his wonderful article "Shakespeare, Shipwrecks, and the Great War: Shakespeare's Reception in Wartime and Post-War Britain," *Shakespeare* 10.3, 2014, Ton Hoenselaars explores the use of tempests and shipwrecks as a metaphor in literature and how these themes function in the context of the playwright's reception during World War I. In the same issue of *Shakespeare*, Monika Smialkowska's "Introduction: Mobilizing Shakespeare During the Great War" examines how Shakespeare's works were used as military propaganda, and Edmund G. C. King's "'A Priceless Book to Have Out Here': Soldiers Reading Shakespeare in the First World War" relates how reading Shakespeare helped British and

Commonwealth soldiers survive the battlefields. *Shakespeare and the Second World War: Memory, Culture, Identity* (Toronto: University of Toronto Press, 2013), ed. Irine R. Makaryk and Marissa McHugh, explores how Shakespeare has framed understandings of World War II since most, if not all, of the combatant powers employed his works for their propaganda. Erica Sheen and Isabel Karremann's collection *Celebrating Shakespeare in Cold War Europe: Conflict, Commemoration, Celebration* (New York: Palgrave Macmillan, 2015) details the influence Shakespeare had on the Cold War and the impact the war had on productions and readings of Shakespeare's plays.

Many authors have written useful studies on pacifism in the literature and culture of the Renaissance. In *The Better Part of Valor: More, Erasmus, Colet and Vives on Humanism, War, and Peace, 1496–1535* (Seattle: University of Washington Press, 1962), Robert P. Adams explores the progression of humanist ideals while cementing his findings in the time period by linking them with figures such as Henry VIII and Cardinal Wolsey. Other studies have explored the ways in which Shakespeare strove to legitimize England's supremacy in his plays. In *Shakespeare's Anti-Politics: Sovereign Power and the Life of the Flesh* (New York: Palgrave Macmillan, 2013), Daniel Juan Gil writes that Shakespeare was anti-political and that his work corrupts the idea of sovereign power to create new selfhood. Heather James, in *Shakespeare's Troy: Drama, Politics, and the Translation of Empire* (Cambridge: Cambridge University Press, 2007), suggests that Shakespeare uses the ideas of Virgil, Ovid, and their contemporaries to fashion a myth about England that he employs to prove the kingdom's legitimacy. Peter Brock's *Pacifism in Europe to 1914* (Princeton: Princeton University Press, 1972) provides a longer view of pacifism throughout history, describing groups ranging from the Czech Brethren of the Middle Ages to the Tolstoyans of 18th-century Russia.

Several studies of Renaissance soldiers have purchase on the topic of pacifism. Adam N. McKeown's *English Mercuries: Soldier Poets in the Age of Shakespeare* (Nashville: Vanderbilt University Press, 2009) maps the works of retired-soldiers-turned-poets in Elizabethan England who provide a different view of war than the patriotic works published in their time do. *Conflict and Soldiers' Literature in Early Modern Europe: The Reality of War* (London: Bloomsbury, 2015), ed. Paul Scannell, delivers a powerful look into the minds of Renaissance soldiers who returned from the battlefield to write about war and the personal trials they faced, whether it be reevaluating religious beliefs or the concept of loyalty. Alan Shepard, in the provocative *Marlowe's Soldiers: Rhetorics of Masculinity in the Age of the Armada* (Burlington: Ashgate, 2002), discusses how Marlowe's plays investigate the nature of war and the role of soldiers.

Other scholars have approached the subject of historical pacifism through discussions of literature. An excellent starting point for European non-dramatic literature is J. H. Hutton's *Themes of Peace in Renaissance Poetry* (Ithaca: Cornell University Press, 1984). Ben Lowe's *Imagining Peace: A History of Early English Pacifist Ideals, 1340–1560* (Pennsylvania: The Pennsylvania State University Press, 1997) investigates the language of peace in Renaissance England by studying historical contexts and written texts in a variety of genres, from fiction to military discourse to sermons. In *History and Warfare in Renaissance Epic* (Chicago: University of Chicago Press, 1997), Michael Murrin takes a new approach to both the history of literature and the history of war through the study of the Renaissance epic. R. S. White's excellent *Pacifism and English Literature: Minstrels of Peace* (New York: Palgrave Macmillan, 2008) surveys works from the Middle Ages to the present day and has an extended discussion of the work of Shakespeare. A much broader but very useful study is John Gittings' *The Glorious Art of Peace: From* the Iliad to Iraq (Oxford: Oxford University Press, 2012), which outlines the arguments for peace made by ancient authors such as Homer before describing ideas articulated by Erasmus and Shakespeare (especially in the later plays).

The field of Peace Studies is vibrant and continues to expand with a number of scholarly journals and several subfields of study. For those seeking to understand the terms of the field, one might begin with Johan Galtung's *Peace by Peaceful Means: Peace and Conflict, Development and Civilization* (London, Thousand Oaks, and New Delhi: SAGE Publications, 1996), which categorizes Peace Studies into four disciplines: peace theory, conflict theory, developmental theory, and civilization theory. Gene Sharp's foundational *The Politics of Nonviolent Action* (Boston: P. Sargent Publisher, 1973) analyzes political power – its creation and its stimulus – through a discussion of the tactics of passive resistance. James Turner Johnson's *The Quest for Peace: Three Moral Traditions in Western Cultural History* (Princeton: Princeton University Press, 1997) examines three traditions in the study of peace as well as the historical details of each: the just war, the sectarian pacifism, and the utopian pacifism. Readers interested in gender studies will find much of use in *Sex and World Peace* (New York: Columbia University Press, 2012), in which Valerie M. Hudson, Bonnie Ballif-Spanvill, Mary Caprioli, and Chad F. Emmett link the security of women with the security of the state. They present their data- and analysis-driven argument and offer approaches to providing security for all. Finally, in his seminal essay "Peace Studies: A Proposal," *New Literary History* 26.3, 1995, Laurence Lerner articulates key tenets of the field and calls upon literary scholars to focus on imaginative texts in order to grant insight into the nature of organized conflict and suggest alternatives.

Index

acting 60
aesthetic drama 58, 62n19, 68
Achilles 28, 79
affect 70, 106, 110n31, 116, 169
Afghanistan 2, 4, 180
Agincourt 9, 71, 152–53
Ahmed, Sara 70, 86n16
Anglo-German Declaration 53
Arendt, Hannah 69, 85n14
Aristophanes 63; *Lysistrata* 63–64, 66
Asimov, Isaac 141, 174n1
astrofuturism 146, 157, 174n15
As You like It, "If" 36, 47–48, 54, 62n16, 62n20, 81, 87, 105, 124, 131; *see also* Shakespeare
Augustine 5, 23

Bacevich, Andrew 7–8, 20, 31n8, 32n32, 181
Bacon, Francis 95, 101, 115, 132; *New Atlantis, The* 115
Ballard, J. G. 160
"band of brothers" 70–71, 118; *see also* Shakespeare
Beckwith, Sarah 9, 31n9, 130, 140n19
Benatar, Pat 63
Berlant, Lauren 71, 86n18
Boston, Bernie 87–88
Branagh, Kenneth: *As You Like It* 56; *Love's Labour's Lost* 75–76; and *Much Ado About Nothing* 36–37; *see also* Shakespeare
Bush, George W. 180

Castiglione, Baldesar 118–19; *Book of the Courtier, The* 119
Central Park 1, 177
Chamberlain, Neville 53–54
Charles I 95
childhood 52
choice 3, 102
Cicero 23
Cold War 146, 150–51
Colet, John 23
colonialism 97, 115
confessions 139n18
conflict 5, 58
constructive storytelling 156
constructivism 12
Cooke, Sam 112
Coriolanus 13–16; and love of war 21; and peace 19–20; and sex 65; *see also* Shakespeare
Costello, Elvis 34–35, 57
courtship 39, 59; *see also* love
Crosby, Stills, Nash, and Young 52
Cupid 79, 98
Cymbeline 183; and harmony 135; and peace 132–36; plots of 131, 134, 138; *see also* Shakespeare

Day of the Lord 61n11
Defoe, Daniel 113; *Robinson Crusoe* 113
Dekker, Thomas 137; *The Wonderfull Yeare* 137
dreams 22, 95, 154, 161, 169–71, 183

Dylan, Bob 108n1, 112, 115–16, 125
dystopias 157–59

Elizabeth I 9–10
emotion 70, 86n16, 104, 111n32, 118, 129–30, 151
Erasmus, Desiderius 86n19, 86n22; and heroism 28–29; and history 173; and human passivity 24; ideal ruler of 27; and peace 25, 28–29, 99, 117–18; and rejection of war 23; and war as unnatural 25
Erasmus, Desiderius (works): "Complaint of Peace Spurned and Rejected by the Whole World, A" 25; 33n42, 118, 139n6; "Dulce bellum inexpertis" 23, 32n37, 33n39, 86n19, 86n22, 176n46; *Education of a Christian Prince, The* 27–30

fairies 91
families 86n19
Farr, Edward, *Beati Pacifici* 137, 140n30
Fiennes, Ralph 13–15, 18
Fletcher, John 65, 85n5; *Two Noble Kinsmen* 85n5; *Woman's Prize, or the Tamer Tamed, The* 65
flower people 88–89, 89
flower power 87–91, 100–101, 105, 107–8
flowers 87–88, 100–101; as nature 104–5
foils 78–79; *see also* swords
forgiveness 9, 139n18
Foucault, Michel 60n3, 185n13

Galtung, Johan 11–12, 20, 32n18–19, 64, 84, 84n2, 84n4, 86n23, 145, 160, 174n13, 190

Gandhi, Mohandas 7, 51
Garson, Barbara 177–78, 180; *MacBird* 177–80
Gaye, Marvin 184; "What's Going On" 184
Gbowee, Leymah 66, 67, 110n26
gender 59; and violence 85n7
Gershwin, George and Ira 76
Ginsberg, Allen 89–90
Golden Age 55, 77, 124
Grady, Hugh 13, 32n22

Hardt, Michael 69, 71, 86n15, 174n8
Harrison, Harry 141–43; "Fragment of a Manuscript" 141–43
Harward, Simon 93
Hawkes, Terence 13, 32n22
Hells Angels 89–90
Henry V 12, 152; and heroism 10; and nationalistic love 70–71; and resolution 9; *see also* Shakespeare
Hercules 74
heroism 10, 28, 94
Hesiod 55
Hitler, Adolf 8
Hoenselaars, Ton 187
Hoffman, Abbie 100–101
Holderness, Graham 9, 31n12
Homonationalism 71, 86n17
Hoover, J. Edgar 178
Huxley, Aldous 156

idleness 7, 14, 19–20, 28–29, 36, 44, 48, 50, 90, 98–99, 105, 107, 121, 124, 158, 168, 182–83
imagination 84, 145
"Imagine" 49, 57, 123; *see also* Lennon, John
Iraq 7, 180
islands 115, 125

James I (of England) 136–38
"Jealous Guy" 49, 61n8; *see also* Lennon, John
Johnson, Lyndon B. 178
"just war" theory 5–6

Kennedy, John F. 178
King, Martin Luther, Jr. 7, 51

Leary, Timothy 89, 108n2
Lebow, Richard Ned 26, 33n44
Lee, Spike 63, 66–68; *Chi-Raq* 63, 66, 68; *Chi-Raq* and peace 83–84
Lennon, John 57, 60n2, 61n8, 108n2, 123, 139n12, 183; *see also* "Imagine"; "Jealous Guy"
Lerner, Laurence 10, 31n15, 190
Loomer, Laura 1
love: and abundance 97–98; and conflict 38, 46; conquers all 73, 77–78; as nothing 39–45; in opposition to war 78; as peace 92; and pretending 99; public vs. private 69–71; *see also* courtship; sex
Love's Labour's Lost: and desire 73–74; ending of 75; *see also* Shakespeare
Lowe, Nick 34, 35

Macbeth 177–78, 180, 183, 184n3, 184n5; *see also* Shakespeare
Machiavelli, Niccolò 22–23; *The Prince* 22–23
"Make Love, Not War" 68–69, 71–72, 74, 82
manhood 70–71, 74, 84
Mars 75, 77–78, 92, 129
Martian, The 114
Mayfield, Curtis 52
memory 52, 62n21, 124, 139n16, 163–64, 168–71, 173, 176n45, 188
Menon, Madhavi 13, 32n24, 99, 110n22

Midsummer Night's Dream, A: and audience 101, 105–6, 108; conclusion of 102–4; and cycle of war 94; and love 95–96; and peace-making 91–92, 106–7; and plague 165–66, 167; and plenty 97; and scarcity 97; as science fiction 141–42; and triumphs 95, 103; *see also* Shakespeare
Montaigne, Michel de 122, 139n13; "Of Cannibals" 122, 139n13
More, Thomas 23, 93, 115, 144; *Utopia* 115, 144
"Mother of All Bombs" 2, 9, 31n2
Much Ado About Nothing 36–37, 76; and Hero's death 43; and love 39–41; and nothing 41–44; and peacetime 38; as problem play 37–38; and romance 44–46; *see also* Shakespeare
Munich Agreement 53

narratives 7, 50; of American conflict 6; and dependence on conflict 18; of love 40; of necessary action 7; Shakespeare's knowledge of 8; of war 30
negative peace 11
Neville, Henry 115; *Isle of Pines, The* 115
New York Workshop in Nonviolence 100
Nobel Peace Prize 3–4, 67
nonviolent action 90–91
North Korea 2, 182

Obama, Barack 145; and *Coriolanus* 18; and history of conflict 21–22; and human history 173; and "just war" theory 5–6, 30; and Nobel Prize speech 3–7, 17; and peace 54

Osborne, John 14
Ovid 124; *Metamorphoses* 124

passive resistance 51
Pax Americana 7–8
Pax Brittanica 53
Pax Romana 53, 131–32
peace: as action 87–89; as
   conclusion of conflict 11; as
   counterpoint to war 10; cyclical
   nature of 93–94; dangers of 18;
   definitions of 11; as goal for war
   6; as ideal 30; as idleness 7, 14,
   28; and imagination 125–26;
   and non-action 7; as a pact
   114; and plenty 133–35; and
   progress 52–53; rejection of
   25–26; and time 60
Peace Studies 9–13, 27, 31n11,
   31n15, 69, 84, 85n9, 90–91,
   109n17, 145, 165, 190
Pepys, Samuel 111n34
performance 77
plenty 30, 36, 48, 93, 96–97,
   109n19, 113, 118, 120,
   123–24, 126, 128, 131–35,
   184
Plummer, Christopher 150
positive peace 11, 14, 156–57
Posobiec, Jack 1
post-apocalyptic novel 158–60
presentism 13, 32n22
problem play 37
protest 25, 66–68, 90–91, 95,
   106, 112–13, 125, 137, 143,
   178–80, 184
Pugliatti, Paola 10, 31n17, 186
Puttenham, George 93

quantification 115

Reagan, Ronald 68
realist 22, 27, 119, 172

realpolitik 22
Rex Pacificus 137
Rich, Barnabe 93
Roddenberry, Gene 147,
   149
romantic comedy 44
Rome 13–14
Rove, Karl 180–81, 183
Royal Shakespeare Company
   (RSC) 76, 146
Russell, J.G. 18

Samson 74
Sanchez, Melissa 65, 84n3
scarcity 92, 97, 120, 123
Schechner Loop 67–68
science fiction 146–47
Serbia 14
sex: in opposition to war 68–69;
   and war 84n4; as war 63–66,
   82; *see also* love
sex strikes 66–68, 76, 85n8,
   85n12, 110n26
Shakespeare, William: and audience
   58–59; and brotherhood
   49–50; and childhood 52; and
   death 47; and empathy 52; and
   inheritance 50, 53, 57; and just
   war 11; and military conflict 10;
   as pacifist 3; and peace 48–49,
   54, 57–58; and peacemakers 50;
   and time 48, 52, 55, 58
Shakespeare, William (works): *As
   You Like It* 36; *Cardenio* 85n5;
   Coriolanus 13–16, 19–20, 65;
   Cymbeline 131, 132–36, 138,
   183; *Hamlet* 38, 110n28,
   149–50, 151–52; *Henry IV* 65;
   Henry V 9, 10, 12, 70–71, 152;
   Henry VI 9; *Henry VIII* 23, 85n5;
   Julius Caesar 1–3, 177; *The Killing
   of King Richard the Second* 177; *King
   Lear* 163–65; *Love's Labour's Lost*

73–74, 75–76; *Love's Labour's Won* 75, 76; *Macbeth* 177–78, 180, 183, 184n3, 184n5; *A Midsummer Night's Dream* 91–92, 94, 95–96, 97, 101, 102–4; 105–8, 141–42, 165–66, 167; *Much Ado About Nothing* 36–37, 38, 39–44, 76; *Pyramus and Thisbe* 102–4, 141–42; *Richard III* 18; *Romeo and Juliet* 72–73; *The Taming of the Shrew* 65–66; *The Tempest* 117–18, 119–21, 122–23, 125–28, 129–31, 153–54, 155–56, 168, 169, 170; *Troilus and Cressida* 18, 79–80, 81–82; *Twelfth Night* 86n21; *Two Noble Kinsmen* 85n5; *Venus and Adonis* 76–80

Sharp, Gene 85n12, 90–91, 109n7, 190
Shirley, James 95
silence 41–42, 44, 116
social drama 58, 62n19, 67–68
soldiers 29, 60n4, 61n7
Spinal Tap 88–89
Stanislavski, Constantin 60, 62n21
Star Trek: The Next Generation 160–62; ending of 153–54; and the future 154–56; and humanity 151–53; Shakespeare in 146–50, 175n19
Star Trek: The Original Series 146–51, 153–57, 161, 165–66, 170, 174n17, 175n19, 175n19, 175nn23–24, 175nn26–27, 175n29
Star Trek: Voyager 166
Star Trek VI: The Undiscovered Country 150–51
Station Eleven 157–58; and fantasy 162–63; and memory 169–70; and Miranda 166–71; and narrative 168–69; and the past 172–73; and plague 165;

structure of 164; and survival 161–62, 165–66; *see also* Mandel, Emily St. John
Stewart, Patrick 146–48
St. John, Mandel, Emily 157–58, 161, 164; *Station Eleven* 157–58, 162–71, 173
storms 116–17, 119–20
Strachey, William 115; *A True Reportory of the Wracke and Redemption of Sir Thomas Gates, Knight* 115
Stradling, John 137
swords 43–44, 51–53, 74, 78
syphilis 82
Syria 55, 61n15

Tacitus 132
Taymor, Julie 128
technology 158, 159
Tempest, The 153–54, 155–56; and audience 129–30; as comedy 129; ending of 125–28; and forgetting 126; and forgiveness 130–31, 170; and grief 127–28; and memory 169; and peace 125; and plenty 122–23, 128; and resolution 168; and rulers 117–18, 124; and scarcity 119–21; *see also* Shakespeare
Third Reich 5
tragedies 60n2, 62
Troilus and Cressida 18; ending of 79–80; and pandering 81–82; *see also* Shakespeare
Trump, Donald 1, 177, 178; and "Make America Great Again" 181; and military strength 182–83; and political violence 2

unhistorical 13, 32n24, 125

Vietnam War 8, 87
violence: desire for 14; against the political right 1
Virgil 77

war: as action 17, 21, 38–40; causes of 26; cyclical nature of 93–94; desire for 17–18; inevitability of 21–22; necessity of 26; rejection of 23; religious argument against 24; and scarcity 96
"War on Terror" 6, 8
Watchmen 87–88

West Wing, The 185n13
White, R.S. 106, 111n33, 189
Wilson, Thomas 137
Women of Liberia Mass Action for Peace 66
wooing *see* courtship
World Economic Forum 144
World Social Forum 143–45
World War I 53–54, 76
World War II 5–6, 30, 75, 181

Zinni, Tony 6
Zizek, Slavoj 55, 61–62n15